PAT BROWN, MBA

Financial Literacy For College Coaches

"How College Coaches Can Win With Money, Protect Their Future, and Lead Beyond the Game"

ABRAM · 47 · BROWN

First edition

ISBN: 978-1-967737-10-9

This book was professionally typeset on Reedsy.
Find out more at reedsy.com

Contents

Introduction: Coaching a New Kind of Game

For years, my mission has been clear: teach financial literacy to student-athletes.

It started as a personal calling—rooted in the realization that young athletes were entering a world of money, contracts, and life-altering decisions without the tools to manage any of it. I saw it in real-time: players earning scholarships, signing NIL deals, even getting drafted—but lacking basic knowledge about budgeting, credit, taxes, or how to turn temporary opportunity into long-term wealth. That's what inspired me to launch platforms like *Financial Literacy For NIL, Financial Literacy For Student Athletes,* and *Financial Literacy For The Culture.*

Through those platforms, I've had the privilege of speaking at schools, connecting with families, and helping student-athletes make smarter moves with their money and their future. I thought that would be my lane—empowering young athletes with the knowledge I wish I had when I was in their shoes.

But then something shifted.

It was a clip of Coach Deion Sanders—Coach Prime—speaking not to his players, but to his staff. He wasn't talking X's and O's. He was talking about **financial literacy**. About making sure his coaching staff understood money, contracts, insurance, and legacy. About educating not just the athletes—but the adults around them.

That moment hit me hard. Because Coach Prime said out loud what many of us in the financial education space already knew: **if the coaches aren't financially literate, how can we expect them to guide the players who**

look up to them?

That moment sparked the idea for this book.

Because the truth is, coaches aren't that different from student-athletes when it comes to money. You deal with the same instability. The same pressure. The same public expectations. The same emotional labor. And, in many cases, the same lack of exposure to financial education.

You've spent your life helping others win—on the court, on the field, in the weight room. You've built programs, shaped lives, and weathered the ups and downs of one of the most demanding professions in the world.

But how much time have you spent preparing for *your own* future? For your family's security? For what happens when the whistle stops blowing?

This book is here to change that.

It's a playbook—not for the game—but for life. For your income, your investments, your contracts, your insurance, and your legacy.

It's designed to give you the same tools and strategies I've shared with athletes, tailored specifically for the coaching journey.

Coach Prime planted the seed. This book is the fruit.

Let's make sure you're not just coaching success—but *living* it.

Because it's time for coaches to win off the field, too.

Why This Book Exists

That moment I watched and listen to a YouTube clip with Coach Prime talking to his coaches that he brought with him from Jackson State to Colorado, Coach Prime didn't just inspire me—it challenged me. It made me look at the bigger picture. Because as I worked with student-athletes, I started to notice something else.

The coaches—the very people tasked with mentoring, guiding, and protecting these young men and women—were often facing the same struggles. Some were navigating short-term contracts and relocations. Others were unsure how their retirement plans worked, how to structure income from summer camps, or how to protect their families financially if something unexpected happened. Some had never been taught the basics of budgeting, investing, or even how to read the fine print of their own employment contracts.

And that's when it became clear:

We can't just stop at educating student-athletes. We've got to equip the people leading them, too.

Which brings us here.

Why This Book Exists

College coaches are leaders. You're strategists, motivators, and program builders. You dedicate your life to developing others—on the field, in the classroom, and beyond. But like many of the athletes you mentor, you may have never been taught how to manage your own money, protect your income, or build lasting wealth.

You're not alone.

This isn't a matter of intelligence—it's a matter of exposure. Financial literacy isn't always passed down. And most coaches, especially those who come from modest beginnings, never had a real opportunity to sit down and learn how money works. You were too busy hustling. Grinding. Building your career one job at a time.

That's what this book is here to fix.

This isn't just a book of financial theory. It's a **playbook**—built specifically for the unique realities of coaching life. We'll talk about managing unpredictable income, understanding your contract, negotiating better terms, consolidating old retirement accounts, and preparing for life after sports—whether that's five years from now or fifty.

We'll also cover how to protect your family, invest wisely, and build the kind of long-term financial security that gives you peace of mind no matter where the next coaching opportunity takes you.

Because financial stability shouldn't be a luxury—it should be your foundation.

And just like you build game plans to win on Saturdays, this book will help you build a financial game plan to win for the rest of your life.

Preface

Coaches are leaders. You inspire, teach, mentor, and develop student-athletes every day—not just in sport, but in life. You preach discipline, preparation, strategy, and execution. But here's a question few people ask out loud:

Who's coaching the coach when it comes to money?

Financial Literacy for College Coaches was written to fill a gap that most never talk about. While you're busy building game plans and raising the next generation of leaders, your own financial future often takes a back seat. Whether you're a head coach at a Power Five program, an assistant grinding at the JUCO level, or a rising star in your early career, the reality is this: **your financial life deserves a playbook, too.**

This book is that playbook.

Inside these pages, we'll talk about the things no one teaches you during the coaching climb—how to manage inconsistent income, how to protect yourself and your family with the right insurance, how to prepare for retirement (even if your schedule barely allows a lunch break), and how to build wealth while you're still grinding.

We'll also dig into topics that hit close to home: what to do with your first big contract, how to navigate job insecurity and relocations, how to invest with purpose, and how to talk to your staff and athletes about money without shame or confusion.

This book is not just about numbers. It's about **freedom, stability, and legacy**. It's about making sure you don't just help others win—you win, too. Because coaching is more than a job. It's a calling. But that calling shouldn't come at the expense of your own financial peace of mind.

So whether you're just starting your journey or looking to tighten up your playbook, this guide is here to walk with you, step by step.

Let's get to work.

— *Pat Brown, MBA*

Former D1 Athlete | Financial Educator | Advocate for Coaches and Athletes

A Quick Note Before You Start

Let me be real with you right from the jump—I'm not a writer. I didn't sit down to craft some perfectly structured, grammatically flawless masterpiece. This book doesn't follow all the "rules" of writing, and honestly, I didn't try to make it fit into any box.

You might catch a typo. You might see a sentence that's a little rough around the edges. And that's okay. Because this isn't about being polished—it's about being **real**.

I didn't write this for critics. I wrote this for coaches.

I wrote it for the assistant hustling to build a future.

For the head coach with a family depending on every contract.

For the ones moving state to state, season to season, trying to stack wins and still find time to think about retirement, insurance, kids' college, or whether the next job will be the last.

I wrote this because too many of us—just like the athletes we coach—were never taught how to manage money, negotiate contracts, or build wealth. We're great at preparing game plans, but nobody ever handed us one for life off the field.

That's what this book is. It's a financial playbook built for **you**.

So if the grammar slips or a line sounds more locker room than lecture hall, give me some grace—and stay focused on what matters: the **message**, the **tools**, and the **real-life strategies** that can help you build the life and legacy you deserve.

Thank you for reading.

And more importantly, thank you for taking your financial life seriously—for yourself, for your family, and for the future.

Let's go get this win.

— Pat Brown, MBA

Part 1: The Coaching Mindset Meets Money Mindset

You already know what it takes to win.

As a coach, you understand structure. You live by preparation. You break down film, run the game plan, and adjust when things get tough. You preach discipline, consistency, and buy-in. You hold players accountable to the system—and you never walk into a game without a strategy.

That mindset? That's what builds championships.

But when it comes to **your money**—are you approaching it the same way?

The truth is, many coaches live in a reactive mode with their finances. They focus on the next job, the next contract, the next season. They grind so hard for everyone else's future, they forget to build their own. And it's not because they don't care—it's because they were never taught how.

Just like many student-athletes, coaches often come from backgrounds where money wasn't talked about. Financial education wasn't offered. And between moving up the coaching ladder, managing a family, and giving everything to the game, there was no pause to learn how to protect what you're earning.

That stops now.

This section is about bridging the mindset you already have as a coach with the mindset needed to win financially. Because once you apply that same discipline, structure, and accountability to your money—you'll realize it's not about how much you make, it's about what you do with it.

Think of it this way:

- **Your playbook = your financial plan**
- **Your game film = your spending habits**
- **Your offseason = your long-term strategy**
- **Your assistant coaches = your financial team (advisor, CPA, attorney)**
- **Your recruiting board = your goals and vision**

You wouldn't build a game plan without reviewing your opponent. So don't build a financial life without understanding the risks. You wouldn't put your players on the field without a system. So don't go into your future without one.

Your coaching mindset is already elite.

Now it's time to bring your **money mindset** up to the same level.

Because whether you're at a Power Five program, a small college, or just breaking into the industry, one thing is true:

You can't lead others confidently until you're leading yourself wisely.

Let's take the same preparation, poise, and process that you bring to every practice—and apply it to your money, your future, and your legacy.

Chapter 1: From Locker Room to Legacy

Coaching is more than a profession—it's a purpose.

You're not just drawing up plays, breaking down film, or managing practices. You're building culture. You're shaping young men and women during some of the most formative years of their lives. You're the mentor, the disciplinarian, the motivator, and the second parent for athletes who may never forget how you made them feel.

You don't clock in and out. You live this.

Coaching is early mornings, late nights, sleepless weekends, and living out of hotel rooms during recruiting season. It's pouring into everyone else, even when your own tank is running low. It's sticking with players when they're struggling—not just on the field, but in life. And for many of you, it's a mission rooted in giving back—because someone once did the same for you.

But while you're investing in everyone else's future, here's the question: **Who's investing in yours?**

Far too many great coaches—some of them championship-winning, nationally respected, well-paid—find themselves unprepared when their career ends. It's not always because they didn't earn enough. It's often because they never had the time, tools, or exposure to build lasting wealth.

You can teach a player to keep their head on a swivel, but have you ever reviewed your own contract line-by-line?

You can lead a film breakdown with surgical precision, but are you tracking your own investments with that same detail?

You'd never let a team enter a game without a plan. So why would you go into the rest of your life without one?

Legacy isn't just what you leave behind on the stat sheet. It's what you leave behind in your bank account, in your family's financial future, and in the freedom you create for yourself once the whistle stops blowing.

The reality is: the coaching carousel is real. Contracts are short. Pressure is high. Job security is fragile—even for the most talented. And in this profession, it's not if you'll face a transition, but **when**.

That's why **financial clarity isn't optional—it's essential.**

It doesn't matter whether you're a head coach at a major program or a position coach grinding your way up the ranks. Without a plan, you're playing defense with your money. And if you're always reacting, you're always behind.

Your players are watching you. Your family depends on you. And your future needs you to think bigger.

From the locker room to your legacy, the habits you build today will shape what life looks like decades from now.

Because one day, the game will end. The locker will be cleaned out. The team will move on.

And when that day comes, will you be able to say:

"I left it all on the field—and I'm financially ready for what's next"?

Let's make sure the answer is yes.

The irony is that many coaches can break down a third-and-long scenario in seconds, but when it comes to things like compound interest, Roth IRAs, or negotiating long-term contract clauses, they're left feeling uncertain—or even embarrassed to ask.

But you're not alone.

Financial literacy isn't something most of us were taught at home, in school, or during our rise through the coaching ranks. It's not part of the coaching certification process. There's no "Financial Fundamentals 101" for assistant coaches moving from DII to D1. And if you're a former athlete-turned-coach, the cycle likely continued: play hard, focus on performance, and let the money figure itself out later.

But later comes fast.

And without preparation, "later" can look like starting over at 55. It can look like trying to catch up on retirement, still renting instead of owning, or feeling unsure about how to help your kids pay for college. It can look like being a highly respected coach—and still struggling behind the scenes.

That's not what your legacy should be.

Your legacy should include options. Ownership. Peace of mind. It should include the ability to take a year off and not panic. It should allow you to walk away on your own terms, not because your financial situation forced you to take a job you didn't want. Your legacy should mean you're in control—not just of your team, but of your life.

Let's also talk about something most coaches rarely admit: coaching is **not stable.**

You could be on a high one season and unemployed the next. Head coaches get fired. Staffs get swept. A single losing season can reshape your entire career. And when those transitions come—and they will—the way you've managed your money will either cushion the fall or intensify the impact.

You may have been told to "keep your head down and work hard," and while that's great advice on the field, it doesn't translate well to long-term financial success. Working hard is important. But so is working smart. And working smart includes knowing where your money goes, understanding how to grow it, and planning for what happens next.

That doesn't mean you need to become a financial expert overnight. You don't need to trade stocks between practices or learn how to write tax code. What you need is awareness, confidence, and the right people in your corner—just like you've always done when building a winning program.

Think about your team for a second.

You don't ask your quarterback to coach the offensive line. You don't expect your trainers to call plays. You put the right people in the right roles, and you guide them with a clear plan.

That same concept applies to your finances. Build a financial "coaching staff." Have a trusted advisor. Find a CPA who understands your unique income structure. Work with an attorney who knows how to read contracts.

And more importantly—**ask questions without shame.**

Because asking now can save you years of struggle later.

From locker room to legacy, this chapter of your career is about more than what's on the scoreboard. It's about freedom. It's about family. And it's about creating something that outlasts the game.

Let's build that, one decision at a time.

Chapter 2: Coaches and Athletes Face Similar Challenges

From the outside looking in, it might seem like coaches and athletes live in two separate worlds. The coach is the leader, the adult in the room, the one with the whistle. The athlete is the student, the learner, the one still figuring things out. But if you peel back the layers—especially when it comes to finances—those worlds aren't so far apart.

In fact, coaches and athletes often face the **same financial challenges**, just in different uniforms.

Let's break it down.

1. Income Volatility

Both coaches and athletes live in performance-based environments where income can change quickly—and sometimes drastically.

For student-athletes now navigating the world of NIL, income can spike unexpectedly from deals, appearances, and sponsorships. But those spikes often come without structure, without taxes withheld, and without any long-term financial plan.

Now look at coaches.

Your income might be steady on paper, but it's often structured with heavy incentives: bowl appearances, win bonuses, camp revenue, performance escalators. One bad season or a staff shake-up can strip thousands off your income. For assistant coaches especially, moving from one program to the next could mean going from a $120,000 salary to $70,000—and back again.

Just like athletes, coaches need to learn how to **build a lifestyle based on their base income**, not their best-case scenario. Anything extra is a bonus—not a foundation.

2. Job Insecurity

Whether you're a redshirt freshman or a seasoned defensive coordinator, the reality is the same: **job security in athletics is fragile**.

Athletes get benched, lose scholarships, or fail to recover from injuries. Coaches get released after losing seasons, new hires, or program overhauls. And sometimes, even success doesn't protect you—budget cuts, changes in leadership, or relocation demands can put you on the move when you least expect it.

That's why financial stability—having an emergency fund, insurance, and an exit plan—isn't just a luxury. It's a necessity.

3. Constant Relocation

Athletes move from high school to college, from state to state for competition, or overseas if they turn pro. They learn to adapt on the fly, pack up their lives, and make new homes quickly.

Coaches know that life all too well.

A coaching career often means moving every few years—sometimes for promotions, sometimes for survival. New cities, new cost-of-living realities, new housing situations, and the strain that constant transition places on spouses and families.

If your financial systems aren't portable—if you don't have digital banking, consolidated retirement accounts, or a nationwide tax advisor—you're left restarting every time you change area codes.

4. Lack of Long-Term Financial Planning

Athletes often live in the now. So do coaches. When the schedule is packed with games, recruiting, practices, and staff meetings, it's easy to say, "I'll deal with it later."

But later rarely comes.

Retirement planning, insurance reviews, investment growth—these are easy to delay when you're chasing wins. But every year you don't plan, you fall further behind.

That's why you can't wait until you're "comfortable" to start planning. Comfort comes **after** the plan is built—not before.

5. Public Pressure and Expectations

Student-athletes are under a microscope now more than ever. Every move is tracked, every mistake is tweeted, and every financial decision they make is scrutinized.

Coaches aren't immune.

Whether you're in front of boosters, dealing with donors, recruiting parents, or speaking to media, your financial image matters. And your players are watching. They see how you move. How you carry yourself. And how secure—or scattered—you are when the conversation shifts from ball to business.

That's why this book exists. To help you build **quiet confidence** in your finances, so you can be the example your players need—without feeling like you have to fake it.

The bottom line is this:

Coaches and athletes may have different roles—but they face the same financial storms.

And just like you wouldn't let a player walk into a game without a game plan, you shouldn't face these challenges without one either.

In the next chapter, we'll start laying the foundation for that plan—by tapping into the mindset you already use every day: your coaching mindset.

Let's shift it toward your finances. You already know how to lead. Now it's time to lead yourself financially.

Chapter 3: Budgeting for the Coaching Lifestyle

Budgeting might not be the sexiest topic in the world, but let's be clear—**it's your financial game plan.** And if there's one thing every coach understands, it's the value of having a plan. Without one, you're just reacting, hoping things work out. And when it comes to money, **hope isn't a strategy.**

Coaching isn't a typical 9-to-5 career. Your income can be inconsistent, your schedule is erratic, and your financial life has to account for things most people never think about: buyouts, bonuses, camp money, relocation costs, postseason incentives, and even sudden unemployment. That's why your budget has to be as flexible and disciplined as your defensive scheme.

Step 1: Know Your Baseline (What You Really Live On)

Many coaches make the mistake of budgeting around their *total compensation*—which may include bonuses, performance incentives, or income from summer camps. But what happens if you miss the playoffs, change schools, or don't host a camp this year?

Your **baseline budget** should be based on your *guaranteed base salary*—the money you know you'll receive every month, regardless of performance. Everything else should be considered "variable" or "bonus" income.

Use that base to determine:

- Monthly bills (mortgage/rent, car, utilities, etc.)
- Fixed obligations (child support, tuition, insurance premiums)
- Essential living expenses (food, gas, medical, etc.)

That number is your **financial floor**—the minimum income needed to maintain your lifestyle. Build your budget from that number, not from best-case scenarios.

Step 2: Account for the Extras (Bonuses, Camps, Stipends)

In coaching, it's common to have extra streams of income:

- Postseason or performance bonuses
- Income from hosting summer camps
- Housing or vehicle stipends
- Speaking engagements or consulting
- Gear and apparel allowances
- Travel per diem reimbursements

Don't build your lifestyle around these. Instead, treat them like "surprise plays"—use them to build wealth, not debt. Great uses for these windfalls include:

- Boosting your emergency fund
- Paying off high-interest debt
- Investing in a Roth IRA or brokerage account
- Making extra mortgage payments
- Setting money aside for tax season

Step 3: Budget for the Offseason and Transitions

Most coaches live season to season—but your budget can't.

During the offseason, your daily schedule changes, travel increases, and income might slow down if your role includes camp money or recruiting-based bonuses. Additionally, job changes can come with sudden gaps in income.

Build a "Transition Fund"—a separate savings account to cover 3–6 months of living expenses. This gives you flexibility if you:

- Lose your job unexpectedly
- Take a new job in a different state
- Need to float expenses between contracts

You don't want to be forced into taking a bad job—or dipping into credit cards—because you weren't financially prepared for the realities of this profession.

Step 4: Use the Right Tools

Today's technology can make budgeting easier than ever. A few coach-friendly tools include:

- **You Need A Budget (YNAB)** – Helps you assign every dollar to a purpose
- **Mint** – Links to your bank accounts to track spending and budgets in real time
- **Rocket Money** – Helps you cancel unused subscriptions and track recurring bills
- **Good old-fashioned spreadsheets** – Simple, reliable, customizable

The best budget is the one you'll actually use. Don't overcomplicate it—just get started.

Step 5: Pay Yourself First

As a coach, you're constantly giving—your time, your energy, your focus. Budgeting gives you a chance to give something back to yourself. Before you pay the bills or upgrade your wardrobe, **automate your savings.** Whether it's $200 a month into a Roth IRA, $500 toward your emergency fund, or $50 into a "vacation with my spouse" account—build the habit.

You've told your athletes a thousand times: *Discipline equals freedom.* The same applies here.

Final Whistle:

Your career may be unpredictable—but your financial life doesn't have to be. A smart, flexible budget gives you power. It gives you peace of mind. It gives you the ability to say no to bad opportunities and yes to the ones that align with your goals.

Budgeting isn't about restriction—it's about control.

And in the coaching world, control is everything.

Chapter 4: Understanding Your Paycheck

The First Step to Controlling Your Money is Knowing Where It Goes

You spend your career teaching attention to detail—run the route crisp, square your shoulders on the tackle, box out with leverage. But when it comes to your own paycheck, many coaches don't take the same approach. They look at the deposit, nod if it "feels right," and move on.

Let's fix that.

Because understanding your paycheck isn't just about knowing what you're making—it's about knowing what's being taken, where it's going, and what opportunities (or liabilities) are hidden in the fine print. You don't need to become an accountant, but you do need to know how to read the financial scouting report—**your pay stub**.

Let's go line-by-line through a typical coach's paycheck and explain what each section means, why it matters, and how it affects your financial future.

Section 1: Gross Pay

Gross Pay is the total amount you're set to earn before anything is taken out. This includes:

- **Base Salary** – Your guaranteed income (e.g., $85,000 annually ÷ 12 months = $7,083/month)
- **Bonuses** – Seasonal or performance-based income, which may be taxable at a higher rate
- **Camp Income** – If run through payroll, this will show up here

- **Stipends** – Monthly or quarterly housing, vehicle, or cell phone allowances

Pro Tip: Just because it's part of your compensation package doesn't mean it's all take-home. The more you understand the breakdown, the better you can budget.

Section 2: Tax Withholdings

Taxes usually take the biggest bite. Here's what you'll likely see:

- **Federal Income Tax** – Based on your income level and filing status
- **State Income Tax** – Varies depending on the state you live/work in (some states have none)
- **Social Security** – 6.2% of your gross pay (up to a wage cap)
- **Medicare** – 1.45% of your gross pay, with no cap

Note: Bonuses are often taxed at a higher "supplemental rate" (~22-37%), so don't expect to take home the full amount.

Section 3: Retirement Contributions

This is where long-term wealth is built—but many coaches overlook it.

- **403(b) or 457(b)** – These are common for employees at public institutions; your contributions reduce your taxable income
- **Employer Match** – Some schools match your contributions up to a certain percentage—this is *free money*, and you should aim to max it out
- **Pension Contributions** – In some states, you'll see mandatory contributions into a state pension plan (e.g., 7.5% to a Teachers Retirement System)

Make sure you know:

- Are you vested in your pension?
- Can you roll your plan over if you switch schools?
- Are your contributions enough to support your goals?

Section 4: Pre-Tax & Post-Tax Deductions

- **Health Insurance Premiums** – Medical, dental, and vision plans often come out pre-tax
- **Life Insurance** – Many schools offer a basic policy; you may pay for extra coverage
- **HSA or FSA Contributions** – Pre-tax savings for health or dependent care expenses
- **Union Dues or Association Fees** – If applicable

These deductions can reduce your taxable income and offer big benefits—*if you're using them strategically.*

Section 5: Fringe Benefits

These are perks that might be taxable or "off-the-books," but still impact your overall financial picture:

- **Housing Allowance or Stipend** – May or may not be taxed depending on how it's structured
- **Use of University Vehicle** – Sometimes taxable as a fringe benefit (especially if for personal use)
- **Gear & Apparel** – Often non-taxable, but could be if sold or heavily personalized
- **Cell Phone or Tech Stipend** – Typically a small monthly reimbursement

Important: If you're receiving fringe benefits, make sure to ask your HR department or CPA whether they'll impact your taxable income. What looks like a perk could also look like income to the IRS.

Section 6: Net Pay (What You Actually Take Home)

After all deductions, what's left is your **net pay**—this is the number that hits your bank account.

Many coaches make the mistake of budgeting off their gross salary. But your lifestyle and spending plan should be built on **net pay**—the money you actually have to work with.

Final Whistle: Know Your Numbers Like You Know Your Roster

Understanding your paycheck isn't about obsessing over every line—it's about taking ownership. You wouldn't go into a game without scouting your opponent. Don't go into life without scouting your finances.

When you understand your paycheck:

- You budget smarter
- You plan with confidence
- You ask better questions during contract negotiations
- And you start managing your money like the professional you are

Because coaching isn't just about wins—it's about building a sustainable life for yourself and your family. And that starts with knowing where your money is going, and making sure it's working for you.

Let's move to the next chapter, where we talk about what happens *after* the check hits your account—and how to prepare for what the game might throw at you next.

Chapter 5: Emergency Funds and Managing Cash Flow

Why Even the Best Coaches Need a Financial Safety Net

If you've been around the coaching game long enough, you know this truth better than most: **things change fast.** One day you're signing an extension, the next day there's a new athletic director with different plans. One season you're headed to the playoffs, the next you're out of a job. You might not even get to finish your coffee before a staff shake-up flips everything upside down.

In a profession built on pressure and unpredictability, there's one financial tool every coach no matter the salary, title, or school size—**must have** in place:

An **emergency fund.**

Not a credit card.

Not a loan from a friend.

Not a "plan to figure it out later."

A real, accessible, purpose-built **cash cushion** that gives you breathing room when life throws a blitz your way.

Why Coaches Need Emergency Funds (Even Highly Paid Ones)

Let's get this out of the way—**being well-paid does not mean you're financially prepared.**

We've seen Power Five coordinators earning six figures who didn't have enough saved to last two months without a paycheck. Why? Because lifestyle often grows as fast as income. Bigger homes, newer cars, private school tuition, travel expenses during recruiting season—it adds up fast. And with short contracts and zero guarantees, there's often no parachute when things go sideways.

Whether you're a GA or a head coach, here's what you're up against:

- Sudden job changes
- Contract non-renewals or buyouts
- Unexpected relocations
- Medical emergencies for you or your family
- Delayed hiring at a new school
- Pay disruptions from athletic department budget cuts

An emergency fund acts as your **financial helmet**—it won't stop the hit, but it can cushion the blow.

How Much Should Coaches Save?

The standard advice for most professionals is 3–6 months of living expenses. For coaches, especially those early in their career or frequently relocating, **aim for 6–12 months.** Here's why:

- Job turnover in coaching is high, even in "good" years
- Relocations may bring temporary double expenses (rent + mortgage, moving costs, hotels)
- New roles don't always come with immediate pay
- Coaching gaps may last longer than expected

Start by calculating your **bare minimum monthly needs**:

- Housing (rent/mortgage, utilities)
- Food and household essentials

- Insurance premiums
- Loan payments (car, student loans, credit cards)
- Family-related expenses (childcare, tuition, medical)

Multiply that number by 6 or 12, and that's your emergency fund goal. You don't need to hit it overnight—but you do need to start building it.

Where Should You Keep It?

Emergency funds should be:

- **Accessible** – You can reach it fast without penalties
- **Safe** – It shouldn't be invested in stocks or crypto
- **Separate** – Not sitting in your checking account where it gets spent accidentally

Ideal places to keep your emergency fund:

- High-yield savings account
- Money market account
- FDIC-insured online savings platform

Keep it boring. This money is not meant to grow—it's meant to **protect**.

Managing Cash Flow Like a Pro

Once you have an emergency fund in motion, the next step is managing your **cash flow**—how money moves in and out of your life.

Coaches often get paid monthly or semi-monthly, and if you're not tracking your bills, subscriptions, camp income, or irregular expenses, things can slip through the cracks quickly.

Here's how to take control:

- **Automate everything** – Bill pay, savings transfers, and retirement contributions
- **Track spending** – Use tools like Mint, YNAB, or simple spreadsheets
- **Create a buffer** – Keep a $500–$1,000 "cash flow cushion" in your checking account to absorb life's random punches (unexpected travel, recruiting meals, etc.)
- **Separate accounts** – Consider different accounts for bills, savings, and discretionary spending

Why It Matters

When you're financially prepared, you coach better.

You think clearer.

You negotiate stronger.

And you sleep easier.

Emergency funds and strong cash flow management won't make you rich, but they will keep you from being **vulnerable**—and in coaching, **stability is power**.

Because when your contract is uncertain, your income unpredictable, and your next job unknown, the only thing standing between you and panic is the plan you put in place today.

So protect your future like you protect your team.

Build your safety net.

And give yourself the freedom to coach with confidence—no matter what the next season holds.

Chapter 6: Investing 101 for Coaches

Turn Your Money Into a Recruit That Works 24/7

You've probably told your players a hundred times: "Don't expect overnight success." Winning takes time, patience, and consistent effort—just like building a strong program.

The same is true for investing.

A solid investment strategy isn't about chasing fast money or playing the stock market like it's a lottery. It's about putting your money to work in a system that builds slowly but steadily, year after year. Just like a freshman redshirt who becomes an all-conference senior, **wealth is built over seasons—not quarters.**

And here's the good news: **you don't have to be a financial expert to start investing.**

You just need to know the basics, stay consistent, and trust the process.

Why Coaches Need to Invest

Your coaching career may not come with guaranteed longevity. Even at the highest level, jobs turn over fast. Raises aren't always promised. Buyouts come with no warning.

You need a plan that:

- Grows even when you're between jobs
- Builds value over time, independent of wins or losses
- Prepares you for retirement, business ownership, or stepping away from

the game

That's what investing does—it gives you leverage over time. It turns the dollars you earn now into passive growth that compounds year after year.

What is Compound Interest?

Compound interest is the financial version of player development.

Let's say you invest $500/month starting at age 30. Assuming a 7% average return, by the time you're 60, you'd have **over $600,000**—even though you only contributed $180,000 out of pocket.

Why? Because your investments earned returns—and those returns started earning returns.

It's not magic. It's math. And the earlier you start, the better the outcome.

Retirement Accounts You Should Know

You've probably heard these acronyms thrown around, but here's what they mean for you:

403(b) Plans

- Offered by public schools and universities (like a 401(k) for educators)
- Contributions reduce your taxable income now
- Grows tax-deferred (you pay taxes when you withdraw at retirement)
- May include employer match—free money if you contribute enough

457(b) Plans

- Also common in public education or government jobs
- Similar to a 403(b), but with fewer penalties for early withdrawal if you leave the job
- Great option if your school offers both—double your retirement saving

potential

Traditional IRA

- Individual Retirement Account anyone can open
- Contributions may be tax-deductible based on income
- Taxes are deferred until you withdraw in retirement

Roth IRA

- Contributions are made with after-tax dollars
- Grows **tax-free**—you don't pay taxes on qualified withdrawals
- Ideal if you expect to be in a higher tax bracket later in life

Pro Tip: If you're early in your coaching career or between jobs, consider opening a **Roth IRA** on your own and contributing what you can. Even $100/month adds up over time.

Simple Investment Strategies for Busy Coaches

You don't need to pick stocks or watch the markets daily. Focus on these fundamentals:

- **Index Funds**: These are collections of stocks that mirror the market (like the S&P 500). They're low-cost, diversified, and consistent performers.
- **Dollar-Cost Averaging**: Invest a set amount every month—rain or shine. This evens out the highs and lows over time.
- **Automate It**: Set up automatic contributions so you invest without having to think about it.
- **Review Quarterly**: Spend 30 minutes every 3–4 months reviewing your accounts. You don't need to obsess—just stay informed.

Where to Open Accounts

If you don't have a retirement plan through your school (or you want to save more), you can open accounts with:

- Fidelity
- Vanguard
- Charles Schwab
- Betterment (automated investing)
- Your local financial advisor or credit union

Common Coaching Mistakes to Avoid

- **Waiting too long**: Don't wait for the "perfect" time. Start small, start now.
- **Ignoring rollovers**: If you switch schools, make sure to **roll over your old retirement plan** so it doesn't get forgotten.
- **Chasing big wins**: Investing isn't like coaching a 2-minute drill. Stick to your game plan and avoid hype.
- **Spending bonuses instead of investing them**: Use performance bonuses or camp income to boost your retirement or emergency savings.

Final Whistle: Treat Your Money Like a Redshirt Freshman

Your money needs time to develop. It won't win today's game—but it'll win the season of life.

Investing isn't about getting rich—it's about **getting free**. Free to walk away when you're ready. Free to provide for your family. Free to coach for purpose, not just for the paycheck.

Start now. Stay consistent. Build wealth like you build a program—one decision, one season, one smart move at a time.

Chapter 7: Understanding Your Retirement Benefits

What You Don't Know Could Cost You Thousands

Let's be honest—most coaches are so focused on developing players and game plans that they rarely stop to read through their own benefits package. Between recruiting, film, practice, and meetings, who has time to dig through HR documents?

But here's the reality: **your retirement plan is one of the most important parts of your compensation package**—and possibly one of the least understood.

Whether you're at a public university, private college, or junior college, your employer likely offers some form of retirement benefit. But if you don't understand how it works—how much you're contributing, how it grows, when it vests, or what happens when you leave—then you could be leaving money on the table.

And in this profession, where job changes are frequent and contracts are short, understanding your retirement benefits isn't just smart—it's essential.

What Type of Retirement Plan Do You Have?

Most colleges and universities offer one or more of the following plans:

403(b) Plans

- Similar to a 401(k), but for educators and non-profits
- You contribute pre-tax dollars from your paycheck
- Grows tax-deferred until you withdraw at retirement
- Many employers offer a match—free money if you contribute enough

457(b) Plans

- Also common in public education and government roles
- Functions like a 403(b), but with an important twist:
- **You can access the money penalty-free once you leave your job**, even if you're under age 59½

State Pension Plans

- Some states enroll coaches and educators into a mandatory pension system
- You and the school both contribute
- Pension amount is usually based on your years of service and final salary
- **Vesting** is critical—more on that below

Understanding Vesting Schedules

Vesting means ownership. It refers to how much of your employer's contributions you're entitled to keep if you leave your job.

- **Employee contributions are always 100% vested**—that's your money.
- **Employer contributions may vest over time**, often 3–7 years.
- If you leave before you're vested, **you may forfeit some or all of the employer match or pension benefits.**

Example: If your plan vests over 5 years and you leave after 3, you might only keep 60% of the employer match.

Action Step: Ask your HR rep:

- What's the vesting schedule on my plan?
- Am I fully vested?
- How many more years until I reach 100%?

Knowing where you stand could make the difference in your decision to leave or stay one more season.

What Happens When You Switch Schools?

Coaching careers are mobile. So what happens to your retirement money when you move?

Option 1: Leave It Where It Is

- Sometimes the easiest option
- Your investments will continue to grow
- You can't contribute anymore, but you'll retain what's yours

Option 2: Roll It Over

- Move it into an IRA or your new employer's plan
- Avoids taxes and penalties if done properly
- Allows you to consolidate and manage all your retirement money in one place

Avoid: Cashing Out Early

- If you take a distribution before age 59½ (or without leaving your job in a 457(b)), you may face:
- A **10% early withdrawal penalty**
- **Income tax** on the entire amount
- Cashing out is rarely worth it—unless it's a financial emergency

Action Steps for Coaches

1. **Find out what type(s) of retirement plan you have**
2. Don't just assume—ask HR for a plan summary.
3. **Log in to your retirement portal**
4. Look at your balance, investments, and contribution percentage.
5. **Increase your contributions if possible**
6. Start with at least enough to receive the full employer match.
7. **Ask about vesting**
8. Know when you fully own the employer's contributions.
9. **Track your accounts**
10. If you've coached at multiple schools, you might have multiple accounts. Don't lose track of old money—**consolidate if possible**.
11. **Meet with a retirement specialist or financial advisor**
12. They can walk you through rollover options, risk tolerance, and long-term strategies.

Final Whistle: Retirement Is Part of the Game Plan

As a coach, you wouldn't dream of heading into the season without a plan. So why treat your retirement like an afterthought?

Retirement may seem like a long way off, but the habits and decisions you make today determine how—and when—you'll be able to walk away from the game on your terms.

Know your plan. Understand your options. Make retirement part of your coaching strategy—because legacy isn't just about wins. It's about freedom. And that starts with knowing how your future is funded.

Chapter 8: Real Estate and Location-Based Decisions

Should You Buy the House—or Just Call the Audible?

One of the biggest financial decisions any coach will make—especially after landing a new job—is whether to **buy a home** or **rent and stay flexible**. The idea of owning property, putting down roots, and building equity is appealing. After all, you've worked hard to get here, and homeownership feels like a natural next step.

But the reality is this: **coaching is a transient profession.**

Your zip code can change every 2–4 years, sometimes less. And while real estate can be an amazing wealth-building tool, it can also become an anchor—financially and emotionally—if you don't play it smart.

Let's break down what every coach needs to consider before signing that mortgage or lease.

To Buy or Not to Buy?

Pros of Buying a Home

- **Equity**: Over time, your monthly payments build ownership in a valuable asset
- **Appreciation**: Homes often increase in value, especially in growing college towns
- **Tax Benefits**: Mortgage interest and property taxes can be deductible

- **Stability**: Owning gives your family a sense of long-term security
- **Control**: You can renovate, customize, and make it truly yours

Cons of Buying a Home (Especially as a Coach)

- **Illiquidity**: It takes time to sell—and you may need to move on short notice
- **Market Risk**: If property values dip or you buy high, you could lose money
- **Maintenance Costs**: Repairs, upgrades, taxes, and insurance can add up fast
- **Emotional Pressure**: Feeling "trapped" in a job or town because of a mortgage
- **Relocation Stress**: Buying and selling repeatedly drains time, energy, and cash

Key Question: Can you see yourself living in the same location for at least 5–7 years?

If not, you may want to rent and remain nimble.

Smart Alternatives for Coaches

University Housing or Stipends

Some schools offer free or subsidized housing for coaches and athletic staff. This can be a huge win—**less financial risk, more savings potential**. If housing is included in your compensation:

- Ask if utilities, maintenance, and insurance are covered
- Bank what you would've paid in rent or mortgage into savings or investments
- Treat it as a short-term boost—not a reason to increase spending elsewhere

Renting vs. Buying

Renting isn't "throwing money away." It's **paying for flexibility**—which may be exactly what you need during a rebuild, probationary period, or while settling into a new community. If you rent:

- Look for lease terms with flexibility (6-month or month-to-month)
- Stay below your housing budget to increase savings
- Keep moving expenses low in case of future relocation

What About Real Estate as an Investment?

Some coaches wisely use their income to **invest in rental property**—either in their college town or elsewhere.

Potential Benefits:

- Passive income stream
- Tax write-offs (depreciation, expenses, mortgage interest)
- Appreciation over time
- Long-term wealth building beyond your salary

But real estate isn't as "passive" as it sounds. It takes:

- Smart location selection
- Understanding property management or hiring a team
- Risk tolerance (vacancies, repairs, tenant issues)

Pro tip: If you do invest, **start small.** Consider a single rental property in a town you know well. Use an LLC to limit liability. And always separate your personal finances from your investment property.

When It's Time to Sell or Stay

If you already own and are considering a move:

- **Run the numbers**: What can you sell for, and what's the net after closing costs?
- **Rent it out**: Could the home become a rental if you're moving temporarily?
- **Don't get emotional**: Homes hold memories—but don't let those outweigh financial logic
- **Talk to a local realtor and financial advisor** before deciding

Final Whistle: Play Smart, Stay Flexible

Real estate can be a powerful tool in your wealth-building playbook—but in a profession where you don't always call the shots on where you live or for how long, **flexibility often beats fixation**.

The key is to treat your housing choice like you treat your coaching decisions:

Analyze. Adjust. Execute.

Whether you rent, buy, or invest, make sure your decision supports your bigger vision—not just your current job. Because one day the job will change—but your financial legacy will still be standing.

Let's keep building.

Chapter 9: Insurance Essentials

Because the Best Coaches Prepare for What They Can't See Coming

In coaching, you preach preparation. You scout your opponents, run walkthroughs, and have backup plans ready. But when it comes to your personal finances, there's one area most coaches overlook—until it's too late.

Insurance.

It's not glamorous. It won't win you Coach of the Year. But it's the single most powerful tool you have to **protect your income, your family, and your future.** Because while you can't always control what life throws at you, you can control whether it destroys what you've built.

Let's break down the five core types of insurance every coach should understand—and how each one acts like your financial defensive coordinator when life sends the blitz.

1. Life Insurance: Protecting Your Legacy

Why it matters: If something happens to you, how will your family maintain their lifestyle? How will your kids go to college? Will your spouse be forced to move, sell assets, or scramble financially?

Types of Life Insurance:

- **Term Life Insurance**
- Coverage for a set number of years (10, 20, 30)
- More affordable
- Great for protecting your family during peak earning years
- **Whole Life or Permanent Insurance**
- Lifetime coverage
- More expensive
- Builds cash value (but often better used as a complement, not your primary strategy)

How much do you need?

At minimum, enough to:

- Pay off debts (mortgage, student loans, car loans)
- Replace your income for 5–10 years
- Fund college or long-term care for dependents

Pro tip: Get coverage *outside* of what your employer provides. If you lose your job, you lose that policy.

2. Disability Insurance: Protecting Your Income

Why it matters: If you get hurt or sick and can't coach, how long can you survive without a paycheck?

Short-Term Disability covers you for weeks or a few months.

Long-Term Disability covers you for years—or even until retirement.

As a coach, your **income is your engine.** If it stops, everything else is affected.

Make sure you understand:

- What your school provides (some offer basic disability coverage)

- Whether you can supplement with a private policy
- How much of your income would be replaced—and for how long

3. Liability Insurance: Protecting Your Career

Why it matters: In an age of lawsuits and social media, **your reputation and job are on the line daily.**

Whether you're accused of misconduct, negligence, or off-field behavior, legal fees alone could drain your savings—*even if you're innocent.*

Types of Liability Coverage:

- **Personal Liability** (usually bundled with homeowners/renters insurance)
- **Professional Liability** or "Errors & Omissions" coverage (sometimes offered through schools or associations)
- **Defamation or reputational protection** for public figures

Pro tip: Check with your school or athletic association about what protection is offered—and what gaps you need to cover privately.

4. Health Insurance: Protecting Your Present

You already know health care is expensive. But do you know:

- What your plan covers *and doesn't* cover?
- How high your deductible is?
- Whether you have access to an HSA (Health Savings Account)?
- What happens to your coverage if you leave or change jobs?

HSA-qualified plans are great for coaches—they let you save pre-tax money for medical expenses, and unused funds roll over year to year.

Make sure your family is covered, too. One medical emergency can derail your financial life *without proper coverage.*

5. Umbrella Insurance: Protecting Your Net Worth

Why it matters: Umbrella insurance is **extra liability protection** that kicks in when your regular policies run out.

Example:

You're sued after a car accident or someone gets injured on your property. Your auto or home insurance covers the first $300,000—but the lawsuit is for $1 million. That $700,000 gap comes out of *your* pocket… unless you have umbrella coverage.

For $200–$400 a year, you can get **$1–$5 million in extra protection.**

If your net worth is growing, this is a *must-have*.

Putting It All Together

Think of insurance like your defensive scheme:

- **Life insurance** protects your family from a financial disaster
- **Disability insurance** protects your paycheck when you can't show up
- **Liability insurance** protects your job and reputation
- **Health insurance** protects your body and bank account
- **Umbrella insurance** protects everything you've worked so hard to build

Final Whistle: You Don't Need to Be Scared—Just Prepared

Coaches spend their careers preparing for every scenario. It's time to apply that same mindset to your finances.

Don't wait for a crisis to figure out your coverage.

Don't assume your employer's policy is enough.

Don't let the unexpected ruin your momentum.

Talk to an advisor. Review your policies annually. Ask hard questions.

Because protection isn't a luxury—it's a legacy move.

In the next chapter, we'll cover how your name, your brand, and your influence are also part of your financial picture—and how to protect those, too.

Chapter 10: Estate Planning for Coaches

When most people hear the term "estate planning," they imagine a wealthy retiree sitting down with an attorney in a glass-walled office. They think of millionaires, sprawling properties, or business tycoons creating trusts for their great-grandchildren. But here's the reality: **estate planning is for anyone who has something worth protecting.**

If you're a college coach, you've already built something meaningful:

- A growing retirement account
- A home you've invested in
- A spouse or partner
- Children who depend on your leadership at home
- Life insurance policies
- A personal brand and network built over years

All of that can be put at risk if you don't have the right plan in place.

This chapter is your wake-up call: **Estate planning isn't about wealth. It's about clarity, control, and care.**

Let's build your legacy together.

What Is Estate Planning?

Estate planning is the process of preparing for the transfer of your assets, the protection of your wishes, and the well-being of your loved ones in the event of death or incapacity. It includes legal, financial, and medical decision-making tools that help ensure your intentions are honored—without leaving a burden behind.

It isn't about focusing on death. It's about preparing for life's uncertainties.

Step 1: Draft a Will

A will is the foundation of your estate plan. It legally states who should receive your assets and who should take care of your children or dependents. It also designates an executor—the person who will ensure your instructions are followed.

Why you need one: Without a will, your assets are distributed according to state law, which may not reflect your wishes. This can cause unnecessary delays, family conflict, and court involvement.

Even a basic will is better than none. Start simple and update as your life evolves.

Step 2: Establish Power of Attorney

There are two main types every coach should have:

- **Financial Power of Attorney**: Appoints someone to manage your finances if you become incapacitated.
- **Medical Power of Attorney (Healthcare Proxy)**: Appoints someone to make medical decisions on your behalf.

Imagine being in a serious accident during a recruiting trip. Who steps in to manage your bank accounts, sign tax forms, or make health care decisions? A Power of Attorney ensures your voice is still heard.

Step 3: Create or Update Your Beneficiary Designations

Many accounts—including your 403(b), 457(b), IRAs, and life insurance—pass directly to the beneficiary listed on the form, not through your will.

Why this matters: If your ex-spouse or an outdated contact is still listed, they will receive the funds, even if your will says otherwise. Coaches with hectic schedules often overlook these details. Don't let that happen to you.

Check and update these designations regularly, especially after life events like marriage, divorce, childbirth, or job changes.

Step 4: Consider Creating a Trust

Trusts are legal structures that hold and manage your assets for the benefit of others. They can:

- Avoid probate (the court process of distributing your estate)
- Provide privacy and protection
- Offer tax advantages
- Protect assets for children or family members with special needs

Types of trusts to consider:

- **Revocable Living Trust**: You control it during your lifetime. It helps avoid probate and allows smooth transition of assets.
- **Irrevocable Trust**: Once established, you can't change it easily. It may offer tax benefits and asset protection.
- **Testamentary Trust**: Created through your will and activated after your death.
- **Special Needs Trust**: Supports a dependent with disabilities without affecting their eligibility for benefits.
- **Charitable Trusts**: Allows you to leave a lasting legacy to causes you care about while reducing estate taxes.

For coaches, a trust can be especially helpful if you have:

- Children from multiple relationships
- A business, camp, or side hustle
- Real estate in multiple states
- A desire to keep financial matters private

Step 5: Write a Living Will (Advance Directive)

A living will outlines your wishes regarding medical treatment if you're unable to communicate.

This can include your preferences about life support, resuscitation, and pain management. In high-stress moments, it spares your family from making heartbreaking decisions.

Combine this with your Medical Power of Attorney for a complete health care plan.

Step 6: Title Assets Properly

Asset titling matters more than most coaches realize. If your home is titled only in your name, it may need to go through probate before your spouse can access it. If your accounts are jointly titled, they may not pass the way you intend.

Work with a financial advisor or estate attorney to ensure:

- Real estate is titled appropriately (consider "joint with right of survivorship" or trust ownership)
- Bank and brokerage accounts reflect your current intentions
- Business interests, trademarks, or digital assets are included

Asset titling can undo a good estate plan if done incorrectly. Don't overlook this step.

Step 7: Organize Your Digital Legacy

More and more of your personal and professional life lives online. Your estate plan should include:

- Login credentials for bank accounts, email, and coaching platforms
- Cloud storage of contracts, NIL content, or team documents
- Instructions for social media accounts and websites
- Digital rights to photos, video content, or branding

Digital estate planning is especially important if your NIL platform or personal coaching brand is part of your long-term income.

Step 8: Communicate and Review Regularly

A perfect plan is worthless if no one knows it exists. Once your documents are signed:

- Store hard copies in a secure place
- Share access with your spouse, trusted advisor, or executor
- Review every 2-3 years or after major life changes

And most importantly: talk to your family.

Let them know where to find things, what your wishes are, and why you've made certain decisions. Clear communication prevents future confusion.

Why Coaches Need Estate Planning More Than Most

Your job is high stress. You travel often. You may move between schools, states, or even countries. You may have income from side work, brand deals, or summer camps. You likely have life insurance, retirement accounts, and some degree of public visibility.

And you likely have people counting on you—financially and emotionally.

All of this makes estate planning not just a good idea, but a responsibility.

Final Whistle: Coach Your Legacy

You build game plans every week. You manage rosters, call plays, and lead people. But your legacy doesn't start and end with wins or titles. It's defined by what you leave behind—not just in memory, but in structure.

Estate planning is your way of staying in control, even after you're gone. It's a final act of leadership. A gesture of love. And a protection plan for the people who matter most.

You don't need to do everything at once. Start with a will. Add a Power of Attorney. Review your beneficiaries. Have the conversation.

The same way you prepare your team for what's next, prepare your family.

Because legacy isn't just what you do on the field. It's what you leave behind when the stadium lights go out.

Part 2: Financial Fundamentals Every Coach Should Know

You've mastered the fundamentals of your sport—technique, repetition, execution. You don't build a winning program by guessing. You build it by focusing on the basics, over and over, until they become second nature.

The same goes for your money.

Before you start worrying about advanced investment strategies, negotiating creative contracts, or building wealth for generations, you need to **master the financial fundamentals**. This is your financial "training camp"—the foundation you'll build everything else on.

And like any good camp, it starts with discipline, clarity, and honest evaluation.

Because the truth is, most coaches don't struggle financially because they're reckless. They struggle because they're busy. They've spent so much time building others that they haven't paused to build systems for themselves.

They're constantly moving—from one season to the next, one city to another, one job to another—without consistent structure around their finances. Paychecks come in, bills go out, and everything else just sort of floats.

But that's not sustainable.

If you want to build lasting financial security—**regardless of your salary, job title, or current circumstances**—you have to commit to mastering the money basics.

In this section, we'll break down:

- How to budget effectively around the unpredictable income and lifestyle of a coach
- Why emergency funds are more than a good idea—they're a lifeline in a profession built on instability
- How to consolidate and organize retirement accounts from past schools and jobs
- What you need to know about cash flow, saving, and paying yourself first
- And how to create a system that gives you peace of mind—not just in your career, but in your personal life

We'll also dive into real-life coaching examples and scenarios. From budgeting around recruiting season and camp revenue, to making sure you don't lose track of retirement funds after switching schools three times in five years, this section gives you the playbook to handle the day-to-day financial realities that come with wearing a whistle.

Remember: fundamentals aren't flashy, but they win games.

You don't need to be a millionaire to start managing your money like one. You just need to get organized, stay consistent, and treat your finances with the same intensity and focus you bring to your team.

This section is your starting point. Let's lay the groundwork for a financial future that works just as hard as you do.

Chapter 11: Tax Planning for Coaches

Coaches don't like surprises—especially the kind that show up in April and come with a five-figure tax bill.

The reality is, coaching is one of the most financially complex professions in higher education and athletics. Between your base salary, bonuses, summer camps, consulting work, media appearances, and maybe even side hustles or NIL work, your income isn't always predictable—and neither is how it's taxed.

This chapter is your guide to understanding, managing, and optimizing your tax life as a coach. Because while you're focused on the scoreboard, what's happening behind the scenes with your taxes could make or break your financial game plan.

Understanding Your Income Sources and Tax Liability

Base Salary Your base salary is typically reported on a W-2 form and taxed just like any employee:

- Federal income tax (based on your bracket)
- State income tax (varies by state)
- Social Security and Medicare taxes

Bonuses (Performance, Signing, Retention) These are taxed as supplemental income. Federal withholding may default to a flat 22%, but depending on your total income, that may not be enough. State withholding varies and may also fall short. You could be under-withheld, creating a surprise bill in April.

Buyouts and Severance Whether you're leaving or being let go, buyouts and severance are taxable in the year they're received. If you receive a large payout without proper tax withholding, it may push you into a higher tax bracket.

Camp Income Running or participating in sports camps can generate significant income—but it often comes via 1099-NEC forms. This income is considered self-employment, meaning you owe:

- Regular income tax
- Self-employment tax (15.3%)

Consulting, Speaking, and Media Work Whether you're advising athletic programs, appearing on sports panels, or running NIL education sessions, these gigs are almost always paid via 1099. That means no taxes are withheld. You must plan for them.

Estimated Taxes: Why and When You Need to Pay

If you have non-W-2 income, the IRS expects you to pay taxes on it as you earn it. These are called **quarterly estimated tax payments** and are due:

- April 15
- June 15
- September 15
- January 15 of the following year

Missing these payments or paying too little results in penalties and interest.

Pro tip: Set aside 25% to 30% of all untaxed income into a dedicated savings account to cover these obligations.

Should You Form a Business Entity (LLC, S-Corp)?

If you're earning more than a few thousand dollars annually from non-salary activities, it may be time to treat your side income like a business.

Sole Proprietorship

- Easiest structure
- No formal registration needed
- File income and expenses on Schedule C of your personal tax return

Limited Liability Company (LLC)

- Offers legal protection
- More professional appearance
- Still files on Schedule C unless you elect S-Corp status

S-Corporation (optional for LLCs)

- Can save on self-employment tax for high earners
- Requires payroll setup and stricter bookkeeping

Benefits of forming a business include:

- Access to more deductions
- Separation of personal and business finances
- Enhanced credibility for consulting and speaking

Consult with a CPA or tax attorney to decide if and when this makes sense for you.

Tax Deductions Coaches Can Claim

If you're receiving 1099 income or operating a coaching-related business, you can deduct legitimate business expenses. Examples include:

- Travel (hotels, airfare, rental cars, mileage)
- Meals while traveling (typically 50%)
- Equipment and supplies for camps or clinics
- Continuing education (certifications, courses)
- Marketing (website, logo design, business cards)
- Home office expenses (if used regularly and exclusively for work)
- Part of your phone and internet bill

Pro tip: Keep meticulous records—digital receipts, mileage logs, and a dedicated bank account can make tax time easier and protect you in case of an audit.

Hiring Help: Why You Need a Coach for Your Finances

Not all CPAs are the same. You need someone who understands the coaching profession—the inconsistent income, the multi-state work, and the nuances of hybrid earners (those who receive both W-2 and 1099 income).

Your ideal tax professional should:

- Understand athletic employment contracts
- Know how to structure and report buyouts
- Help plan for large income years (bonuses, book deals, etc.)
- Anticipate future growth (you may go from assistant to head coach quickly)

Think of your CPA as your defensive coordinator—they read the field and keep you out of trouble.

Dates Coaches Should Know

- **January 15**: Final estimated tax payment for the prior year
- **January 31**: Deadline to receive W-2s and 1099s
- **February 28**: Deadline to issue 1099s (if you pay others for work)
- **April 15**: Tax Day (filing deadline and 1st estimated tax payment)
- **June 15**: 2nd estimated tax payment due
- **September 15**: 3rd estimated tax payment due
- **October 15**: Final deadline if you filed an extension

Staying ahead of these dates helps you avoid penalties, maximize deductions, and lower stress.

Other Smart Tax Strategies for Coaches

1. Max Out Retirement Contributions

- Contribute to your 403(b), 457(b), or IRA to lower taxable income
- Consider a SEP IRA or Solo 401(k) if you run a business

2. Use an HSA (Health Savings Account)

- Triple tax advantage: tax-deductible contributions, tax-free growth, tax-free withdrawals for medical expenses

3. Track State Residency

- If you work or move across state lines, you may owe taxes in multiple states
- Keep a log of where you live, vote, and work to determine residency for tax purposes

4. Defer Income (When Possible)

- Talk to your employer about timing bonuses or payouts strategically
- Defer compensation into retirement or annuity plans if offered

Final Whistle: No Surprises

Just like your pre-game preparation sets the tone for performance, **your tax planning sets the tone for your financial security**.

Understand your income. Track your expenses. Ask smart questions. Partner with the right professionals. And never let taxes become an afterthought.

Because in this game, the coach who plans ahead keeps more of what they earn.

And that's how you win—on and off the field.

Chapter 12: Running Camps, Consulting, and Speaking Engagements

Turn Your Coaching Expertise Into Smart, Structured Income

You've spent years developing systems, building relationships, and mastering the art of teaching. You've built a playbook, a philosophy, and a leadership style that not only wins games but also changes lives.

Now here's the big question: **Have you ever considered that what you know is marketable?**

As a coach, your expertise is in high demand. Whether it's hosting summer camps, offering one-on-one consulting to programs in need of help, or speaking at clinics and conferences, you have opportunities to earn additional income—**if you treat your knowledge like a business.**

This chapter is all about showing you how to **structure your skills into income**, stay compliant with tax laws, and make the most of your side opportunities without creating a financial mess.

The Opportunity: How Coaches Monetize Their Skill Set

Here are a few common ways coaches can earn extra income:

1. Summer & Offseason Camps

- Host individual or team skill development camps
- Invite youth programs, high school athletes, or position-specific groups
- Charge registration fees and sell branded merchandise

2. Consulting for Teams & Coaches

- Help new programs build culture, systems, or game plans
- Offer film analysis, recruiting evaluations, or staff development
- Provide virtual or in-person sessions

3. Speaking Engagements

- Share your story at coaching clinics, conferences, or community events
- Speak on leadership, resilience, or player development
- Record and sell online workshops or masterclasses

These are not only great ways to earn income but also powerful tools to **build your brand, extend your influence, and make an impact beyond your current program.**

Structuring It: Sole Proprietor vs. LLC

If you're earning money outside of your employer's W-2 income, you're technically a **business owner**. And that means you need to choose the right structure for your side hustle.

Option 1: Sole Proprietor

- Easiest and fastest way to get started
- No formal registration needed in most states
- You report your income and expenses on **Schedule C** of your personal

tax return

Pros: Low cost, simple setup

Cons: No legal protection between your personal and business assets

Option 2: LLC (Limited Liability Company)

- Separates your personal assets from business liabilities
- Requires registration with your state and a small annual fee
- You can still report taxes as a sole proprietor or elect to be taxed as an S-Corp if income grows

Pros: Legal protection, more credibility, easier to expand

Cons: Slightly more paperwork and costs

Pro tip: If you're earning more than $10,000 annually from side income, consider an LLC to protect yourself and set a professional tone.

Tracking Income and Expenses

No matter which structure you choose, you need to treat your side income like a **real business**—and that starts with bookkeeping.

Track All Income:

- Registration fees (camps, clinics)
- Speaking honorariums
- Digital product sales
- Consulting fees
- Sponsorships or partnerships

Track All Expenses:

- Facility rental fees
- Equipment and supplies
- Travel costs (mileage, airfare, hotel)
- Marketing materials (website, flyers, social media ads)
- Meals during travel
- Insurance for liability at events

Use tools like:

- QuickBooks Self-Employed
- Wave (free accounting software)
- Excel or Google Sheets
- A physical ledger—if you prefer old-school methods

Keep all receipts and categorize them clearly. At tax time, you'll be able to reduce your taxable income through legitimate business deductions—saving you thousands of dollars.

Setting Up Business Bank Accounts

Open a **separate bank account** for your side income. This will:

- Keep your business and personal money separate
- Make tracking and taxes 10x easier
- Present a more professional image for vendors and clients

Comply with Your Employer's Rules

Before you start promoting your camp or consulting brand, **check with your athletic department or university HR**. Some institutions have guidelines about outside income, use of school logos, or facility rental.

If you're upfront and transparent, most schools are supportive—especially if you're enhancing the university's brand or bringing in positive attention.

Final Whistle: You're Not Just a Coach—You're a Business

Every successful program starts with a vision, structure, and consistent execution. The same goes for your side income.

You don't need to "go big" to start. Just go smart.

Run your camp with clarity. Offer your consulting services with confidence. Accept speaking engagements with professionalism. And build something that grows over time.

Because when you treat your expertise like a business, your reputation builds, your income diversifies, and your financial security expands—one opportunity at a time.

Chapter 13: Planning for the Career Arc

Prepare Financially for Every Step of the Coaching Journey

Coaching isn't just a job—it's a journey. From grinding as a graduate assistant to leading as a head coach, or eventually stepping into athletic administration or academic roles, every step comes with new opportunities, challenges, and financial realities.

The key to lasting success—**on and off the field**—is recognizing that your financial needs, responsibilities, and goals will change along the way. What works for you at age 28 might not work at 48. And what's manageable as an assistant can become risky when you're in charge of a program and a payroll.

This chapter is about **seeing the big picture**, planning ahead, and staying financially ready—no matter where your coaching path takes you.

The Early Years: GA, Intern, or Entry-Level Assistant

These years are all about hustle, sacrifice, and earning your stripes. Financially, they're often the leanest—and also the most dangerous, because poor money habits formed now can carry into higher-earning years.

Key Goals:

- **Budget with discipline**—live below your means
- **Build your emergency fund**—at least 3–6 months of expenses
- **Start investing early**, even small amounts (Roth IRA, 403(b))

- **Avoid lifestyle creep** when you get that first big raise
- Track **student loans** and consider long-term repayment strategies

Mindset shift: Don't think of this as "survival mode." Think of it as **foundation-building mode** for your financial future.

Middle Years: Position Coach, Coordinator, or Recruiting Specialist

Now you're earning more, building a reputation, and likely starting a family or buying a home. But with more money comes more responsibility—and more opportunities to spend without thinking.

Key Priorities:

- **Maximize retirement contributions** (especially if your school offers a match)
- **Track your vesting schedule** for pensions or 403(b)/457(b) plans
- **Start estate planning**—will, life insurance, beneficiaries
- **Plan for relocation flexibility** (don't overcommit to real estate)
- **Consider side income** opportunities: camps, speaking, consulting
- **Protect your income** with disability and umbrella insurance

Career tip: Get clarity on contract terms like buyouts, bonuses, and housing stipends—these affect your real compensation and tax planning.

Peak Years: Head Coach, Administrator, or Leadership Role

Now you're in charge. Your income is likely at its highest, but so is the pressure. These years are about **preserving what you've built** and creating the ability to walk away *on your terms.*

Financial Focus:

- **Diversify income**—investments, real estate, businesses
- **Work with a trusted financial advisor** to manage assets and cash flow
- **Consolidate retirement accounts** from prior schools/employers
- **Optimize tax strategy**—use CPAs familiar with athletics and multi-state income
- **Negotiate smart contracts**—consider deferred comp, retention bonuses, insurance perks
- **Involve your spouse or partner** in long-term planning conversations

These are also the years when you should **start visualizing what comes next**. You may love the game, but don't let it be your only plan.

The Transition: Life After Coaching

Whether you retire early, pivot to another role, or are forced to step away due to burnout or family needs, the transition out of coaching is inevitable. The question is: *will you be ready for it financially and emotionally?*

Common Paths After Coaching:

- Athletic Director or administrative leadership
- Teaching or faculty role in sports management
- Entrepreneurship (camps, clinics, training businesses)
- Media, broadcasting, or public speaking
- Consulting for other programs or athletic departments
- Private sector leadership (nonprofits, youth sports, brand partnerships)

Financial Considerations:

- **Will your retirement savings cover your new lifestyle?**
- **Do you need to downsize or adjust spending?**
- **Are your benefits portable?** (health insurance, pension access)
- **Do you have a new income stream—or a plan to create one?**
- **Have you built a professional network you can activate post-coaching?**

Planning for Early Retirement or Sabbaticals

Some coaches step away before age 60—by choice or circumstance. That's where **financial independence planning** matters most.

How to Prepare:

- Use **tax-advantaged accounts** but also build **after-tax savings** for flexibility
- Know your school's **early retirement policies**
- Understand **Social Security rules** and **Medicare timelines**
- Consider **working part-time** or consulting to bridge the gap

Final Whistle: Think Beyond the Season

You coach your team to improve every year. Your financial plan should evolve too.

Wherever you are on the coaching arc, now is the right time to:

- Assess your position
- Define your next step
- Prepare for a future with options

Because your career is a journey, not a job—and the best journeys are built with purpose, preparation, and a plan that goes all four quarters... and beyond.

Chapter 14: Supporting Family Without Overextending

Care for Others Without Compromising Your Financial Future

Coaches give.

You give your time, energy, guidance, and support to your players, your staff, your community—and, often, to your **family.** Whether it's helping aging parents, supporting children through school, or giving a hand to siblings or extended relatives, many coaches find themselves playing a financial role outside of their immediate household.

And while it's honorable to help your loved ones, here's the hard truth:

You can't pour from an empty cup.

This chapter is about learning how to **support your family without sacrificing your future.** It's about setting boundaries, making intentional choices, and keeping the long game in mind—even when emotions are involved.

The Reality: You Might Be "The One"

In many families, especially if you've achieved a certain level of success, you become "the one" people look to when things get tough.

- "Can you co-sign this loan?"
- "We just need help with rent this month."
- "Can you cover Mom's prescriptions?"

- "Your niece is applying to college—can you help with tuition?"

The pressure is real. It comes from a place of love, but also from expectation. And if you don't set clear limits, it can **quietly derail your financial plan.**

Before You Give: Ask These Questions

1. **Can I afford this without dipping into my emergency fund or retirement savings?**
2. **Will this impact my ability to pay for my own children's needs or future goals?**
3. **Is this a one-time gift or an open-ended obligation?**
4. **Am I enabling someone's poor financial habits—or empowering them to grow?**
5. **What would happen if I said no?**

Sometimes helping means **saying yes with structure**. Other times, helping means **saying no with love.**

Create a Family Giving Plan

Just like you create a game plan for Saturdays, create a **giving plan** for your family life.

- **Set a yearly giving budget**: Decide how much you can give or gift without disrupting your goals
- **Build a "Family Fund" savings account**: Contribute to it monthly, so you have money ready for birthdays, emergencies, or planned support
- **Decide who qualifies**: Immediate family only? Parents? Siblings? Be specific
- **Discuss with your spouse or partner**: Get on the same page and commit to a united front

Setting Boundaries With Love

It's possible to be **generous and wise** at the same time.
Here's how to say "no" without guilt:

- "I want to help, but I've already allocated my giving budget this quarter."
- "I'm working with a financial plan and need to stick to it."
- "I'm happy to give advice or help you create a budget, but I can't contribute financially right now."
- "Let's talk about a plan that empowers you to become more financially stable."

Remember: **saying no to someone else may be saying yes to your own kids, spouse, or peace of mind.**

When You Do Decide to Help

If you choose to assist financially:

- **Give without expecting repayment**, unless you create a formal loan agreement
- **Use written agreements** for larger commitments
- **Set timelines and limits** ("I'll help for 3 months," "Up to $1,000 only")
- **Encourage financial education**—help them grow, not rely

Pro tip: Instead of recurring handouts, consider offering to pay for **tools that build independence**—budgeting apps, credit counseling, financial literacy resources, or job training.

The Hidden Impact on Coaches

Supporting others financially can also lead to:

- Emotional burnout
- Marital tension
- Delayed retirement
- Resentment if relationships become one-sided

You wouldn't run your program without discipline, structure, and communication—**your finances deserve the same.**

Final Whistle: Be Generous, But Be Strategic

There's nothing wrong with wanting to help your family. In fact, it's part of what makes you a great coach—a natural provider, protector, and problem-solver.

But you must remember: **you're building something too.**

A future for your own household. A retirement you've earned. A legacy your kids can count on.

Support with wisdom.

Set boundaries with grace.

Lead your family by example—not by overextending yourself until you can't lead anymore.

Because true generosity comes from a place of strength—not sacrifice.

Chapter 15: Building Wealth That Outlasts the Game

From Paychecks to Freedom, From a Career to a Legacy

You've spent your life in the grind—early mornings, late nights, film sessions, road trips, and recruiting wars. You've worked for every dollar, climbed every rung, and earned every promotion.

But what happens when the whistle blows for the last time?

What happens when the paychecks stop?

Most coaches are taught to chase the next opportunity, the next salary bump, the next title. But the real win—**the ultimate win**—isn't just earning a bigger paycheck.

It's building **wealth that works while you sleep.**

It's creating a life that continues to pay you long after your final game.

It's having the freedom to say "yes" because you want to—not because you have to.

This chapter is about moving from **paycheck-dependence to financial independence**, and from income survival to **wealth that outlasts the game.**

Step One: Define Financial Independence

Financial independence means you have enough income—from your investments, savings, pensions, or businesses—to pay your bills and live your lifestyle **without needing a job.**

It doesn't mean you stop working.

It means you stop working **because you have to.**

Financial independence gives you options:

- Take a sabbatical
- Step away from toxic work environments
- Start your own business
- Spend more time with family
- Volunteer, travel, or explore passions beyond the game

It's not about being rich.

It's about being **in control.**

Step Two: Shift from Earned Income to Investment Income

Your paycheck is earned income—it stops when you do.

Wealth comes from **investment income**—it keeps growing even if you're not on the clock.

Types of investment income:

- **Stocks and index funds** (capital gains, dividends)
- **Real estate** (rental cash flow, equity appreciation)
- **Business income** (camps, clinics, training academies, consulting)
- **Pensions or annuities**
- **Royalties or content platforms** (books, courses, videos)

Your goal:

Gradually **reduce dependence** on your job and increase what your money is doing *for you.*

If your investments can eventually replace your paycheck, **you're free.**

Step Three: Build for Generational Wealth

It's one thing to build financial freedom for yourself.

It's another to create a legacy that lives on after you.

Generational wealth means:

- Your kids don't start from zero
- You pass down assets—not just debt
- Your values, work ethic, and wisdom are reinforced through financial structure

How to create it:

- Invest in **real estate** that can be passed down
- Open **Roth IRAs or 529 plans** for your children
- Purchase **life insurance** to create liquidity for your heirs
- Set up a **will, trust, or estate plan**
- Teach your children **financial literacy early**
- Document your financial journey so they can learn from your wins and mistakes

Money alone isn't a legacy.

Knowledge + structure + money is how you change a family tree.

Step Four: Live Life on Your Terms

Imagine waking up and doing what you want—not because a contract says so, but because your life is built on purpose and planning.

That could mean:

- Starting a nonprofit or mentoring young coaches
- Taking a role you love, even if it pays less

- Writing a book, starting a podcast, or launching a brand
- Moving closer to family or finally buying that lake house
- Spending uninterrupted time with your kids or grandkids

You don't have to wait until retirement age to design your ideal life.

You just have to start building the foundation now.

Final Whistle: You've Been Coaching a Team—Now Coach Your Legacy

Your players come and go. Your titles and trophies are great—but **your real legacy is what you leave behind for your family, your community, and yourself.**

Building wealth that outlasts the game isn't about status. It's about **freedom. Impact. Control. Peace. Options.**

You've helped others win your whole career.

Now it's time to make sure you win—**for life.**

Part 3: Growing Wealth Like You Build a Team

Long-Term Strategy, Compound Success, and Playing the Financial Long Game

Coaches are builders.

You recruit talent, install systems, develop culture, and refine your program one season at a time. You don't expect instant results—but you know that if you stay consistent, keep showing up, and execute the plan, success will come.

That same philosophy applies to **building wealth**.

Growing wealth isn't about hitting one big payday. It's not about guessing the next hot investment or banking on your next raise. It's about putting a long-term system in place—a plan that grows steadily, adjusts when necessary, and builds toward something bigger than this season or even this job.

And here's the key: **You already know how to do it.**

You know what it takes to:

- Recruit the right pieces (your financial team)
- Develop depth (multiple income streams)
- Train with intention (invest consistently)
- Protect your starters (insurance & estate planning)
- Coach with a vision (set long-term goals and execute)

This section will help you take that coaching mindset and apply it directly to your financial future.

We'll dive into:

- **Investing 101**: Understand how your money can work for you—even while you're asleep or on the recruiting trail
- **Retirement Plans**: Learn how to maximize 403(b)s, 457(b)s, IRAs, and pensions—even if you've worked at five schools in the last ten years
- **Real Estate and Equity Building**: Explore how to make smart decisions with home buying, relocations, or investing in rental property
- **Multiple Income Streams**: Discover ways to grow your wealth beyond your coaching salary—through camps, consulting, speaking, content creation, and more
- **Long-Term Goal Setting**: Build a vision for the next 10, 20, or 30 years—so you're not just earning, but building something that lasts

Whether you're coaching at a JUCO, a mid-major, or a top-tier program, wealth-building is within reach. It doesn't take millions. It takes **discipline, consistency, and a clear plan**.

The same way you build a winning team—recruiting, developing, executing—you can build financial security that frees you and your family to make decisions based on purpose, not panic.

This isn't about getting rich quick. It's about building a life where you don't have to look over your shoulder. A life where you can leave the game on your own terms, knowing that the wealth you've built will continue to serve your family long after the final whistle.

Let's dig into the fundamentals of growing wealth—*the same way you've always built your programs: one smart decision at a time.*

Chapter 16: Understanding Your Coaching Contract

Read the Fine Print Before You Sign the Bottom Line

You've worked your whole life to get here—interviews, recommendations, performance, and reputation. Now you've landed a coaching job, and the offer is on the table.

But before you celebrate or sign, it's time to understand what you're really agreeing to.

Your coaching contract isn't just a job offer—it's a legal, financial, and professional roadmap.

If you don't understand the terms, you may find yourself stuck, exposed, or short-changed later.

Let's break down the most common terms in coaching contracts and what they really mean.

Base Salary vs. Incentives

- **Base Salary**: This is your guaranteed pay. It's what you earn annually, typically paid monthly or biweekly.
- **Incentives**: These are bonus payments tied to performance. Examples include:
- Winning season bonus
- Playoff or bowl game bonus
- Academic performance of athletes

- Conference or national recognition
- Retention or contract renewal bonuses

Tip: Understand whether incentives are taxed at a higher rate, and don't budget your life around income that isn't guaranteed.

Buyout Clauses

This is one of the most important parts of your contract.

- **If You Leave**: A buyout clause may require you to pay the school (or forfeit future earnings) if you exit the contract early.
- **If They Terminate You**: A buyout clause will determine how much the school must pay you if you're fired **without cause**.

Watch for:

- Prorated buyouts (the amount owed decreases over time)
- Offset clauses (reduces what the school owes if you get a new job)
- Language that defines "cause" very broadly (can eliminate your payout)

Length of Term

This defines how long the contract is valid—typically 1 to 5 years.

Key points:

- **Short-term deals** may offer flexibility but little security
- **Longer-term deals** give more protection but might include steeper buyouts
- Pay attention to **termination language**—can they fire you at will or only under specific conditions?

Conduct Clauses

These are morality or behavior clauses that allow the school to terminate your contract **with cause** for personal conduct that damages the program or institution.

Examples of triggering events:

- Legal trouble or arrests
- NCAA violations
- Public scandals or social media issues
- "Conduct unbecoming" or vague language

Tip: If the clause is too broad or subjective, it can be used to fire you without a buyout. Get legal clarity if needed.

Renewal Language

This section covers what happens at the end of your contract term.

- Is renewal automatic?
- Does it require mutual agreement?
- Is there a performance trigger tied to renewal?
- When will you be notified about renewal?

Tip: Know the timeline for renegotiation—and make sure it gives you time to plan for your next move if things go south.

Perks and Non-Salary Benefits

Coaching contracts often include valuable extras beyond your paycheck:

- **Vehicle**: Use of a university or sponsored car, or a monthly stipend
- **Housing**: Either provided housing or a monthly housing allowance

- **Travel**: Per diems or reimbursements for recruiting or event travel
- **Camp Income**: Do you keep 100% of what you make from running camps? Is it split with the school?
- **Tickets, Gear, Tech**: Football tickets, branded apparel, laptops or phones
- **Spouse Travel or Family Benefits**: Paid travel for bowl games or events

Tip: While perks are great, they may have **tax implications**. Some are considered "fringe benefits" and may be taxable.

Final Whistle: Get Professional Eyes on It

Before signing any contract:

- **Consult a sports attorney** or agent
- **Have a CPA or financial advisor review the compensation package**
- Make sure you understand the risks and the protections

You'd never let your players compete without knowing the rules.

Don't let yourself step into a contract without knowing your rights.

This isn't just a coaching deal—it's your **livelihood, your leverage, and your legacy.**

Chapter 17: Countering and Negotiating Creatively

Build the Deal That Works for Your Life—Not Just Their Budget

The job is exciting. The opportunity is big. The offer is on the table.

Now what?

Most coaches—especially early in their careers—treat a coaching offer like it's final: take it or leave it. But the truth is, **everything is negotiable**. And the more you understand how contracts work, the more confident you can be in **shaping a deal that serves your long-term goals, not just your short-term title.**

Even if you're not at the Power Five level, you still have leverage—especially if you bring value, have a unique skillset, or are being pursued by multiple programs.

Here's how to counter and negotiate **smartly and creatively.**

Retention Bonuses: Rewarding Longevity

You're being hired to build something—but what happens when you succeed, and others come calling?

What to Ask For:

- **Annual retention bonus** for staying beyond each contract year
- **Milestone bonuses** (e.g., $10,000 after 3 years, $25,000 after 5)
- **End-of-contract lump sum** if you complete the full term

Why it matters: It rewards loyalty and protects you from constant lateral moves just to get a raise.

Performance-Based Raises: Tie It to Results

If you believe in your ability to win, let that confidence show in your contract.

Examples:

- Automatic raise after a winning season
- Salary bump tied to playoff appearance, bowl game, or team GPA
- Bonus pool increases for staff after program milestones

Why it matters: It sets you up for compensation growth without having to renegotiate every time you succeed.

Health and Retirement Benefits for Family

Don't overlook the **real value** of benefits. A slightly smaller salary can be offset by **better support for your family**.

What to Ask For:

- **Health coverage for your spouse and children** (including dental/vision)
- **Employer retirement contributions** to a 403(b) or 457(b)

- **Dependent care stipends** for childcare
- **Tuition assistance or tuition exchange** if you're at a private institution

Why it matters: These benefits directly affect your family's well-being—and often go untouched in initial offers.

Protect Your Income in Case of Termination

This is non-negotiable. **Every coach needs a strong buyout clause.**

What to Ask For:

- **Guaranteed payout** of remaining salary if terminated without cause
- **No "offset clause"** (or a favorable one), so your buyout isn't reduced if you take another job
- **Clear definition of "cause"** that protects you from vague terminations

Why it matters: In coaching, the question is rarely *if* you'll be fired—it's *when*. Get your parachute in writing now.

Final Tip: Negotiate Structure, Not Just Salary

If the school can't meet your number, shift the conversation:

- Ask for more perks (housing, car, travel)
- Request camp income rights or revenue share
- Propose deferred compensation or signing bonuses
- Suggest professional development or coaching clinic budgets

Think long-term. **Smart structure > shiny salary.**

Chapter 11: Innovative Contract Examples

Learn from the Best—and Adapt Their Tactics to Your Career

When people hear about big-time coaching contracts, they usually only see the headlines: "$5 million per year," "$1M signing bonus," or "10-year deal."

But behind the numbers are **creative strategies** that smart coaches and agents use to build security, flexibility, and legacy.

Let's look at three well-known coaches who've structured their contracts *strategically*—and how you can use similar ideas at your level.

John Harbaugh (NFL Head Coach, Baltimore Ravens)

Key Strategy: Deferred Compensation & Supplemental Retirement

- Harbaugh negotiated **deferred payments**, meaning some of his income is paid later—often tax-deferred
- He uses **supplemental annuity plans** to grow retirement assets in low-tax years
- His deal includes **long-term financial planning tools** baked right into the contract

Takeaway for You:

Ask if your school can contribute to a **403(b)**, **457(b)**, or **supplemental retirement account**. You can also defer bonuses to later years when your tax bracket may be lower—or structure bonuses to hit in separate calendar years to reduce the tax burden.

Dawn Staley (Head Coach, South Carolina Women's Basketball)

Key Strategy: Equity-Based Bonuses & Purpose-Driven Pay

- Staley's contract includes **bonuses tied not just to wins, but also to program equity**, including student-athlete graduation and DEI impact
- Her deal contains **escalating bonuses** for reaching deeper rounds in the NCAA Tournament
- She negotiated **long-term investment into the program's growth**, not just personal income

Takeaway for You:

Tie performance pay to **your unique value**—team GPA, community engagement, diversity initiatives, or building a culture. Don't be afraid to **redefine what success looks like**, especially at programs that are rebuilding.

Juwan Howard (Head Coach, Michigan Men's Basketball)

Key Strategy: Insurance-Backed Compensation & Long-Term Guarantees

- Howard incorporated **insurance-based vehicles** (like cash-value life insurance or annuities) to create **tax-advantaged wealth**
- His deal includes **multi-year guarantees** that extend even beyond active coaching years
- It also includes **benefits for his family**, such as post-retirement coverage

Takeaway for You:

Even if your income is modest, you can:

- Ask for **long-term disability insurance**
- Request **life insurance contributions** as part of your contract
- Explore **split-dollar insurance plans** with a financial advisor if you're

at a higher income level

Adapting Big-Time Ideas to Any Level

You don't need to coach in a major conference to think creatively.

Here's how to bring it down to your level:

- Ask your school to pay for **an annual financial planner** to help with taxes and investments
- Structure part of your camp income as a **business entity** and negotiate facility use agreements
- Request **tuition waivers or employee benefits** for graduate programs or your spouse
- Include a **professional development fund** for clinics, courses, or certifications

Final Whistle: Build Contracts Like You Build Game Plans

Your contract should reflect your **value, your strategy, and your vision**.

Don't just accept what's offered—shape it.

Don't just ask for more—ask for *smarter.*

And most of all, make sure every deal you sign brings you closer to the **freedom, stability, and legacy** you've been working so hard to earn.

Because coaching is what you do.

But smart negotiation?

That's how you **win for life.**

Chapter 18: Long-Term Career Strategy and Retirement Planning

D*on't Just Finish Strong—Finish Free*

Most coaches spend their entire careers planning for the next season, the next job, the next opportunity. But far fewer spend time planning for the final chapter—the moment when they walk away from the sideline for good.

And that's a problem.

Because one day, the whistle will blow for the last time. The question is: **will you be ready?**

This chapter is about building your **long-term strategy**—financially, professionally, and personally. It's about creating a blueprint not just for success during your coaching years, but for freedom and fulfillment after them.

Let's look at the four most common long-term pathways for college coaches—and how to prepare for each one financially and strategically.

1. Administrative Transitions: From Coach to Athletic Leader

For many coaches, the natural next step is into **athletic administration**—becoming an athletic director, associate AD, or transitioning into compliance, development, or academic services.

Why it makes sense:

- You stay connected to athletics and mentorship
- You gain a more predictable schedule and workload
- You build influence in shaping entire athletic departments

How to prepare:

- Pursue graduate education or certifications (e.g., sports management, leadership)
- Volunteer on administrative committees or strategic planning groups at your current school
- Network with other administrators across departments
- **Plan for a pay shift**—some admin roles may pay less than head coaching positions
- Maximize retirement benefits and negotiate carry-over of leave, insurance, and pension credits

Financial Strategy: Use your peak coaching years to stack retirement contributions and eliminate debt, so you can pivot with more flexibility.

2. Early Retirement: Freedom on Your Terms

Some coaches step away by choice in their 40s or 50s, ready to travel, spend more time with family, or simply enjoy life without the pressure of recruiting and game days.

How to prepare:

- Know your **financial independence number**—the amount of savings/investments needed to retire early
- Build up **after-tax investment accounts**, not just tax-deferred retirement funds (you'll need penalty-free access before age 59½)

- Consider **retirement healthcare costs**, especially if stepping away before Medicare eligibility at 65
- Look into **401(k)/403(b) catch-up contributions** if you're 50+
- Consider **downsizing your home**, relocating, or changing your spending lifestyle gradually

Financial Strategy: Prioritize saving 25–35% of your income during your peak earning years. Use compound interest and diversified investments to buy back your time later.

3. Business Ownership: From Coach to CEO

Whether it's running a training academy, starting a consulting firm, launching a recruiting service, or opening a gym—many coaches dream of turning their passion into a business.

Why it's a great fit:

- You already have leadership skills and a network
- You understand branding, operations, and team-building
- You can scale your influence outside the school system

How to prepare:

- Start small while you're still coaching (speaking, online courses, camps)
- Form an **LLC or S-Corp** to separate business and personal finances
- Work with an attorney to handle contracts, waivers, and liability
- Build your business plan *before* you step away from coaching
- Save 6–12 months of personal and business expenses before launching full-time

Financial Strategy: Treat your business like an asset—invest in it, track it, protect it, and build it with systems that don't rely 100% on your presence.

4. Financial Independence: The Endgame

Ultimately, the goal is simple: **you want options.**

Whether you work, consult, volunteer, or travel, financial independence means:

- You don't have to take a job just for the money
- You can retire when you want, not when you're forced out
- You have the freedom to say *yes* or *no* based on values—not bills

How to achieve it:

- Know your monthly lifestyle cost and build a retirement income plan to match
- Diversify income streams—retirement accounts, rental properties, investments, annuities
- Reduce or eliminate all debt by your mid-50s
- Keep insurance and estate planning updated
- Stay financially literate and involved in your own plan

Financial Strategy: Build toward a life where *work becomes optional*—and fulfillment becomes your full-time job.

Final Whistle: Build the Exit You Deserve

Every coach has an end game. The ones who win are the ones who plan for it early.

Start today:

- Map out your long-term career path
- Clarify what "freedom" looks like for you and your family
- Talk to professionals who can help you build a strategy
- Invest consistently—not just in the market, but in your skills, your brand,

and your network

Because your coaching journey may have started on the field...
But your legacy is built **long after you leave it.**

Part 4: Protecting the Coach, the Brand, and the Family

Because Winning Means Nothing If You Can't Keep It

You've spent your whole career helping others win.

You've built programs, poured into athletes, and worn your school colors with pride.

But now it's time to talk about something most coaches put off for too long: **protection**.

Because it's not just about how much money you make—it's about how much you keep.

It's about what happens if the game changes, the job disappears, or life throws you something you didn't see coming. And it's about making sure that what you've worked so hard to build **doesn't crumble** under stress, loss, or a lack of planning.

This part of the book is all about safeguarding the things that matter most:

- **You** – your income, your health, and your ability to coach
- **Your brand** – your reputation, your name, and your off-field business potential
- **Your family** – the people who've been in your corner through every season, every move, and every win or loss

We'll dive into:

- The essential **insurance coverage** every coach should have
- How to protect your income from injury, illness, or early retirement
- The basics of **estate planning**—because yes, coaches need wills too
- The impact your financial life has on your **spouse, children, and future**
- Why protecting your name and reputation is part of building your financial brand
- How to keep control when life feels out of your control

Here's the truth: a lot of coaches avoid these topics because they're uncomfortable. Talking about death, disability, or worst-case scenarios doesn't come easy. But the most successful coaches don't just prepare their teams for best-case outcomes—they plan for the bad breaks, too.

If you've ever told your players "protect the ball," then you already know where we're going.

Your money, your brand, your health, your future—**they're all the ball.**

And it's time to protect them with the same urgency you bring to 4th-and-1.

Because coaching is only part of your identity.

Your legacy—what you build, what you protect, what you pass on—that's the endgame.

Let's make sure it's secure.

Chapter 19: Navigating Job Changes and Relocations

One of the least predictable aspects of a college coaching career is job security. Unlike many traditional careers, coaching contracts are often tied to win-loss records, recruiting results, and administrative or institutional shifts. Even the most talented and respected coaches may find themselves transitioning unexpectedly—whether by choice or circumstance. That's why understanding how to navigate job changes and relocations from a financial perspective is essential to long-term stability and peace of mind.

This chapter explores how to plan for career transitions, handle the financial implications of buyouts or terminations, manage moving stipends, and make smart tax-related decisions when crossing state lines.

Job Security Is Never Guaranteed

In coaching, your current position could end due to a losing season, a staff shakeup, or a new athletic director wanting to bring in their own team. Even if you're excelling, the nature of the profession means you should always be prepared to move—geographically and financially.

Rule of Thumb: Build an emergency fund with at least 6-12 months of living expenses to cushion you during gaps in employment or between contracts.

Understanding Buyouts and Terminations

If you're terminated from a position, your contract may include a buyout clause or severance agreement. These payouts can be substantial, but they also come with complexities.

Key Points to Review in Your Contract:

- Is there a buyout clause, and how is it calculated?
- Are severance payments subject to non-compete or confidentiality clauses?
- How are benefits like health insurance handled post-termination?

Tax Note: Buyouts and severance payments are considered taxable income and may bump you into a higher tax bracket. You may want to work with a CPA to spread the tax impact over time or increase withholding accordingly.

Relocation and Moving Stipends

If you accept a new position in another city or state, the institution may offer a moving allowance or reimbursement. While helpful, these stipends often come with reporting requirements.

Important Considerations:

- Many moving stipends are considered taxable income unless you're in the military (as of the current U.S. tax code).
- Track every expense, including receipts for movers, housing, travel, and meals.
- Understand the deadline for submitting expenses and what qualifies under your institution's HR policy.

Pro Tip: Consider negotiating your relocation package before signing your contract. Clarify whether it's a reimbursement, a fixed stipend, or handled through direct billing.

State Tax Implications of Moving

Every state has different income tax laws. Moving from a no-tax state (like Texas or Florida) to a high-tax state (like California or New York) can significantly impact your net income.

Before You Move:

- Run a side-by-side income comparison, factoring in state income tax, cost of living, housing, and benefits.
- Check your new state's rules on residency, partial-year taxation, and tax credit eligibility if you're earning income in multiple states.

After You Move:

- Update your payroll and tax withholding forms.
- Notify the IRS and your financial institutions of your address change.
- Consider adjusting your budget or salary negotiations to offset any increased tax burden.

Housing Considerations and Market Volatility

Relocating often means selling one home and buying or renting another—sometimes under pressure. Market conditions, timing, and your contract's start date may impact your choices.

Tips for Coaches in Transition:

- Avoid buying a new home immediately unless you're confident the job is long-term.
- Negotiate for temporary housing assistance or paid housing during the transition.
- If you own property in your old location, consult a real estate advisor about whether to sell or rent it out.

Supporting Family Through the Move

Your spouse or partner may need to change jobs. Your kids may be switching schools. Emotional support and logistical planning are just as important as financial preparation.

Suggestions:

- Include family relocation services in your negotiation package.
- Discuss the move with your family early and often.
- Budget for visits back to your former home, school fees, or transitional childcare.

Final Thoughts

Job changes and relocations are part of the coaching life. They don't have to derail your financial progress—if you plan ahead.

When you view each job offer as both a professional and financial contract, you protect your income, your lifestyle, and your peace of mind. Work with a financial advisor to evaluate opportunities from every angle and prepare your personal finances for whatever lies ahead.

Because in the world of coaching, it's not a matter of *if* you'll move—it's a matter of *when*. And when that time comes, the most successful coaches won't just have a new whistle ready. They'll have a relocation budget, a tax plan, and a long-term vision, too.

Chapter 20: Spouses and the Coaching Journey

Your Career Isn't Just Yours—It's a Family Mission

When you accept a coaching job, you're not the only one stepping into a new role. Your spouse, your children, your entire household becomes part of the journey. The wins, the moves, the uncertainty, the pressure—it impacts all of you.

The truth is, **coaching is a lifestyle—not just a job.** And that means your financial decisions can't be made in a vacuum. They must be made together, as a family team.

This chapter focuses on how to strengthen your partnership—**not just in marriage, but in money.** Because if you want to build real, lasting wealth and freedom, your spouse needs to be in the huddle, not on the sidelines.

Plan Together: Your Family is Your First Team

Coaches are often natural leaders, used to making quick calls and big-picture decisions. But when it comes to your household finances, leadership doesn't mean control—it means **collaboration**.

Whether your spouse manages the day-to-day household or has a demanding career of their own, you both deserve to understand and shape your financial game plan.

Key strategies:

- Hold **monthly money meetings**—review income, expenses, and goals
- Share passwords, account access, and investment statements
- Make budgeting a **family exercise**, not just a spreadsheet
- Talk openly about **what money means** to each of you—security, freedom, legacy, peace of mind

The goal isn't just wealth—it's alignment.

Prepare for Job Transitions: Stay Ready So You Don't Have to Get Ready

In coaching, transitions are part of the game. A great season may lead to a promotion; a bad one might lead to a pink slip. Either way, **your family needs stability when your career doesn't offer it.**

How to prepare:

- Build a **6- to 12-month emergency fund**—especially important in short-term contracts
- Know your **buyout terms** and what your spouse needs to know if you're terminated
- Keep a **moving budget**—anticipate the cost of relocating for the next opportunity
- Involve your spouse in **contract discussions** and **career planning**
- Maintain **portable benefits** when possible (independent life insurance, Roth IRAs, etc.)

Have a "what if we had to move tomorrow?" checklist. If your spouse is caught off guard, it creates more stress than any game ever could.

Build a Shared Vision of Wealth and Freedom

What's the point of winning games if you can't win in life?

It's easy to stay focused on the next recruiting class or next season's depth chart—but without a shared financial vision, your family may spend years surviving instead of thriving.

Define your shared goals:

- Do we want to retire early—or slow down our work years in our 50s?
- Do we want to own property in a "forever place," even if we move often?
- Do we want to build wealth for our kids, for causes we care about, or to live more freely?
- What does **freedom** actually look like to us as a couple?

Create your **household mission statement**—not just for your coaching philosophy, but for your life philosophy. Use that to shape your decisions around investing, saving, spending, and giving.

Final Whistle: You and Your Spouse Are the Real Team

In every program, success depends on communication, strategy, and unity. The same is true at home.

Your spouse is more than just your support system—they're your partner in building a life that's not defined by job titles or win-loss records, but by **purpose, security, and shared joy.**

You don't just coach a team.

You lead a household.

So bring your spouse into the huddle.

And call plays that you both believe in—for the long run.

Chapter 21: From Coach to Connector – Helping Your Athletes Win with NIL

By now, you've walked through budgeting, investing, taxes, contract language, retirement planning, and building long-term wealth. You've looked at how to protect your income, how to create multiple streams, and how to plan beyond the current job.

But here's the real kicker: **you're not just a coach—you're a multiplier.**

Everything you've learned in this book? You can now pass on to your athletes. And in this new world of Name, Image, and Likeness (NIL), they need your leadership more than ever.

Because talent will get them in the door. But financial literacy? That's what helps them **stay in the game after the lights go out.**

Why Coaches Are Crucial to NIL Success

You're on the front lines. You're in the locker room. You know your players' backgrounds, their family situations, their dreams—and their blind spots.

Many student-athletes are navigating sudden income, public exposure, and contract decisions with zero preparation. And while NIL is a powerful opportunity, it also comes with **financial landmines** that can derail a promising future.

That's where you come in—not as their agent, but as a trusted **mentor, guide, and connector**.

How to Support Your Athletes with NIL Opportunities

1. Promote Education First

- Recommend financial literacy resources (books, courses, podcasts, apps)
- Host a "Money Monday" team meeting once a month
- Bring in local CPAs, financial advisors, or former players to speak
- Encourage athletes to take ownership of their earnings—not hand it off blindly

"If they can learn the playbook, they can learn the paycheck."

2. Encourage Smart NIL Partnerships

- Help them think long-term: Is this deal building their brand, or just giving them short-term cash?
- Push them to ask: "Does this align with who I am on and off the field?"
- Introduce them to alumni or local businesses looking for authentic ambassadors
- Teach them to **evaluate contracts**: exclusivity, deliverables, termination clauses

A $500 NIL deal that damages their reputation isn't worth it. Teach them to protect their name like a logo.

3. Connect Them to Professionals

- Keep a trusted list of vetted CPAs, NIL attorneys, insurance reps, and advisors
- Help them understand the difference between an agent and a financial planner
- Offer to attend meetings with them—not as a negotiator, but as a support figure

Empower your athletes to build a "financial team" like they have a coaching staff.

4. Show Them How to Use NIL to Fund Their Future

- Help them set aside a portion of every deal for savings or investing
- Introduce them to the concept of compound interest and long-term growth
- Encourage them to use NIL to start a business, fund grad school, or support their families **without going broke**
- Teach them how taxes work and why they need to track their earnings

NIL shouldn't be a flex—it should be a foundation.

How to Spot When an Athlete Needs Help

- Sudden spending with no plan
- Reluctance to talk about money
- Asking vague questions about taxes or contracts
- Leaning too much on friends or family "advice"
- Confiding in you but unsure how to move forward

Sometimes, just asking:

"Hey, do you need help figuring that out?"

...can be the difference between a smart decision and a regret.

Be a Bridge, Not Just a Coach

You don't need to be a financial expert.

You don't need to handle their money.

You just need to be the **bridge** that connects them to people and resources that will help them grow.

You already teach discipline, character, and hard work. Now add

financial confidence to that list.

Final Whistle: Leave a Legacy That Lasts

The athletes you coach may forget the stats. They may forget the final score. But they will never forget the life skills you taught them along the way.

By helping them understand NIL—not just as a trend, but as a tool—you give them the chance to **win at life**, not just on game day.

And that's what coaching is really about.

You've built your playbook. Now help them build theirs.

You've secured your financial future. Now help them believe theirs is possible.

That's leadership.

That's legacy.

That's what this next generation needs.

And you're ready.

Part 5: Taxes, Business Opportunities, and Coaching Income Streams

Maximize Your Earnings, Minimize Your Surprises, and Diversify Your Game

When people hear "college coach," they often think of one paycheck. One school. One salary.

But anyone who's been in the profession knows it's rarely that simple.

You might have a base salary from your university, but it's likely only part of the story. You could be earning camp income, appearance fees, stipends, performance bonuses, housing allowances, media gigs, or side consulting work. You may even be picking up income from online courses, youth coaching, or speaking engagements.

That's a lot of moving parts.

And if you're not managing those streams wisely—especially when it comes to taxes—you could be leaving money on the table or walking into an IRS nightmare.

The truth is, every dollar you earn is a business decision—whether you treat it like one or not.

This section of the book will give you the tools to:

- Understand your tax obligations and avoid painful surprises in April
- Structure your side income legally and smartly
- Explore additional income streams based on your coaching expertise
- Learn how to protect your time, reduce liability, and build financial

freedom
- Use your unique skill set to create opportunities off the field

Because yes, you're a coach—but you're also a **brand, a mentor, and a business.**

And the more you treat yourself like one, the more financially stable, versatile, and empowered you become.

We'll cover:

- How coaching bonuses and camp income are taxed
- What deductions you can take as a coach (yes, there are some!)
- Whether or not you should form an LLC for your speaking, training, or consulting work
- How to legally and efficiently track income and expenses
- Strategies for building multiple streams of income while staying focused on your main job
- The importance of record-keeping, quarterly tax payments, and working with the right CPA

You don't have to become an accountant or a tax pro. But you do need to know enough to protect your income, avoid costly mistakes, and make the most of your expertise.

Because your paycheck is just the beginning.

Let's explore how to turn your coaching skills into a complete financial ecosystem—one that supports your family today and builds opportunity for years to come.

Chapter 22: Multiple Streams of Income for Coaches

Build Beyond Your Contract and Create Options for Life

As a coach, you know better than anyone—**no job is permanent.** One losing season, a new athletic director, or budget cuts can turn your world upside down. That's why relying on just one income source (your salary) can be risky.

But here's the good news: **you have more to offer than you may realize.** Your experience, voice, and leadership hold value far beyond the sidelines—and there are many ways to turn that value into additional income.

This chapter is about expanding your earning potential through **diversified income streams**, not just to survive job transitions—but to **build wealth, freedom, and long-term options.**

Why Multiple Streams of Income Matter

- **Security**: If one stream dries up, others keep you afloat
- **Freedom**: More income means more choices—where you work, how long you work, and what you walk away from
- **Legacy**: Extra income can fund long-term goals—college savings, retirement, generational wealth
- **Growth**: Every income stream you build is an opportunity to grow professionally and personally

In short: **Your income should reflect your full potential—not just your job title.**

1. Youth Camps & Clinics

One of the most common (and powerful) ways for coaches to generate additional income is through **camps** and **clinics**.

Opportunities:

- Position-specific skill camps (e.g., QB clinics, shooting camps, etc.)
- Team or youth development camps during school breaks
- Specialized coaching sessions in underserved areas or niche sports
- Coaching clinics for other professionals or high school staff

Pro Tips:

- Structure the camp as a **business** (LLC or sole proprietorship)
- Keep records of expenses (facility rental, staff, gear, insurance) for tax deductions
- Check with your university on camp revenue policies and facility use
- Market your camp using social media, local networks, and alumni lists

2. Coaching & Leadership Consulting

You've developed systems, culture, and leadership philosophies that others can learn from. Why not monetize it?

What You Can Offer:

- Team-building workshops for schools, clubs, or corporate groups
- One-on-one consulting with new coaches or administrators
- Program evaluations for struggling programs or youth organizations

- Online or in-person leadership seminars

Pro Tips:

- Start small—offer one workshop, gather testimonials, then scale
- Charge per session, per project, or on a retainer basis
- Create PDF guides or digital toolkits as part of your consulting service

3. Public Speaking

Your story matters. Your journey, your setbacks, your triumphs—they all teach valuable life lessons. Public speaking allows you to **inspire, educate, and earn**.

Where You Can Speak:

- Coaching clinics and sports conferences
- Leadership seminars
- High school or college assemblies
- Faith-based events or men's groups
- Business conferences looking for motivational speakers

Pro Tips:

- Develop 2–3 signature talks and practice them well
- Build a simple speaker bio and rate sheet
- Record a short demo video to share with event organizers
- Don't be afraid to start free and scale as your brand grows

4. Online Courses & Training Content

We're in the era of **digital knowledge.** Coaches can now turn their expertise into **online products** that sell 24/7.

What You Can Create:

- Position-specific drills or playbooks (video or eBooks)
- Culture-building or leadership mini-courses
- Video breakdowns of offensive/defensive systems
- Courses for aspiring coaches or student-athletes

Platforms to Consider:

- Teachable, Kajabi, or Thinkific for full online courses
- Patreon or YouTube for monthly subscribers
- Gumroad or Payhip for downloadable products

Pro Tips:

- Start with one simple resource—a video series or PDF workbook
- Promote through your network, social media, or LinkedIn
- Focus on **what people are always asking you for**—turn answers into income

5. Social Media & Brand Partnerships

Coaches with strong online presence and credibility can explore:

- Sponsored posts (from sports gear or training brands)
- Affiliate marketing (sharing products with a commission)
- Branded content or appearances

Even if you're not a "social media person," you can still **build influence** through blogging, podcasts, or sharing useful content consistently.

Legal and Tax Considerations

Before you build these streams:

- Check your contract for outside income restrictions
- Track **every dollar earned** and **every expense incurred**
- Consider forming an **LLC** for protection and tax efficiency
- Set aside 25–30% of side income for taxes (or pay quarterly estimates)
- Work with a CPA familiar with athletics and entrepreneurship

Final Whistle: You're More Than a Coach—You're an Entrepreneur

You don't need to be famous. You don't need a national platform.

You just need **value**, a **willing audience**, and the **discipline to build** something outside your job.

Your job pays the bills.

Your multiple streams build your freedom.

So start today. Pick one income stream to test this year. Use what you already know to create something new.

Because when you stop thinking like just a coach and start thinking like a brand—you unlock possibilities that can last a lifetime.

Chapter 24: The Coaching Ladder – Financial Moves for Every Stage

No two coaching journeys are the same—but every coach moves through stages. From the GA who's barely scraping by to the head coach negotiating seven-figure extensions, your income, responsibilities, and financial decisions evolve at every step.

The key? **Matching your financial strategy to your career stage.**

Because if you treat your money like it's temporary, you'll always be broke. But if you approach each phase with intention and preparation, you'll build a foundation that lasts long after the final whistle.

Let's break it down.

Stage 1: The Graduate Assistant (GA)

"I'm getting paid in gear and meals... barely."

As a GA, you're hustling. Long hours, low pay, and probably carrying some student loan or credit card debt. It's easy to feel like financial planning can wait—but this is the **most important time** to build discipline.

Financial Focus:

- **Live like you're broke—because you are.** Don't inflate your lifestyle, even with stipends or free perks.
- **Start tracking every dollar.** Use a simple budget (Mint, Rocket Money,

Google Sheets) to get clear on what's coming in and going out.

- **Build a $500–$1,000 emergency fund.** Just one surprise expense can throw you into panic.
- **Pay off high-interest debt** if possible. If not, at least avoid adding more to it.
- **Learn now.** Read, watch, and study financial literacy while your plate is light financially but heavy with time.

Discipline with $500 a month turns into wisdom with $5,000 a month.

Stage 2: The Position Coach (Newly Promoted or Hired)

"I finally got a real paycheck—now what?"

You just landed your first "real" job. Maybe you've gone from making $10K to $60K+. It's tempting to celebrate with a new car or apartment upgrade, but now's the time to **build the habits that create long-term freedom.**

Financial Focus:

- **Don't jump straight to lifestyle creep.** Keep living like a GA for 6–12 more months.
- **Automate savings.** Put 10–15% into a high-yield savings or Roth IRA right off the top.
- **Start investing.** Open a Roth IRA, or enroll in your employer's 403(b)/457(b).
- **Build a 3–6 month emergency fund.** This will give you stability if staff changes happen.
- **Start tracking your net worth.** Knowing your money is power.

The biggest financial mistake at this stage is living up to your paycheck instead of ahead of it.

Stage 3: Assistant Head Coach or Coordinator

"I'm making real money now—it's time to think bigger."

Your pay is up. Your responsibility is up. And the pressure? Definitely up. This is where your financial decisions start having long-term impact.

Financial Focus:

- **Meet with a financial advisor or CPA.** You've got more money now—make sure it's protected and growing.
- **Max out retirement contributions.** Hit the ceiling on your 403(b), 457(b), and Roth IRA if possible.
- **Start investing beyond retirement.** Brokerage accounts, index funds, real estate—get your money working.
- **Check your insurance.** Long-term disability, life, liability—protect your family and your name.
- **Start thinking legacy.** Estate planning, wills, and trust conversations should begin here.

*You're no longer just earning income. You're building **leverage.***

Stage 4: Head Coach

"I'm running the program—and the business behind it."

At this point, you're a CEO in a whistle. Contracts, media, boosters, legal exposure, staff hires—all of it runs through you.

Now your financial decisions impact not just your life—but your family, your staff, your athletes, and your long-term legacy.

Financial Focus:

- **Hire a full team: financial advisor, CPA, attorney, estate planner.**
- **Negotiate every contract with long-term protection.** Focus on:
- Buyouts
- Deferred compensation
- Retention bonuses
- Guaranteed years
- Performance escalators
- **Create multiple streams of income.** Speaking, consulting, online platforms, real estate, NIL guidance, etc.
- **Evaluate contracts every 1–2 years.** Even if you're not moving, keep leverage.
- **Plan succession and retirement.** What happens if you leave tomorrow? What happens if you stay 10 more years?

> *A head coach without a financial plan is just borrowing success from the present—and risking everything for the future.*

Key Contract Questions to Ask at Every Level

- Am I building long-term financial security—or just chasing the next job?
- Do I understand my contract language (buyouts, benefits, perks)?
- Is my family protected if something happens to me or my job?
- Am I using this stage to set up the next one?
- What does *freedom* look like for me—and how am I building toward it?

Final Whistle: Build a Plan That Outlasts the Job

Coaching careers are unpredictable. But your financial life doesn't have to be.

No matter where you are on the ladder—just starting out or managing a national powerhouse—you have a choice: survive each season or **build something that lasts beyond it.**

Your legacy isn't just wins and banners.

It's security.

It's options.

It's wealth.

It's peace.

So coach, whatever level you're at—start planning like you'll be promoted, and saving like you might be fired.

That's the real game.

And it's one you can absolutely win.

Chapter 25: Navigating Burnout, Pressure, and Financial Decisions

How Mental and Emotional Fatigue Affects Financial Clarity—and Tools to Reset and Refocus

College coaching is more than a job—it's a lifestyle. The schedule is demanding. The expectations are relentless. The stakes feel personal. You're expected to win, develop young people, lead your staff, navigate recruiting, and represent your program with integrity, 24/7. Add to that the emotional load of your personal life, and it's no surprise that many coaches experience **burnout**—a chronic condition of physical, emotional, and mental exhaustion.

But here's something we rarely talk about: **burnout doesn't just affect your performance on the field—it affects your decisions with money.**

This chapter is about learning to recognize how **pressure and fatigue** can cloud your financial judgment and how to use tools and strategies to **reset, refocus, and make smart financial choices**, even when the emotional tank feels empty.

The Silent Influence of Burnout on Money

Burnout isn't just about being tired—it's about being **depleted**. And when you're depleted, your decision-making ability takes a hit.

Think about it: when your body is running on fumes and your mind is overstimulated, you're more likely to:

- Avoid important financial decisions entirely
- Procrastinate on reviewing contracts, insurance, or investments
- Overspend to self-soothe (retail therapy, spontaneous getaways)
- Overcommit financially to please others
- Under-prepare for long-term needs like retirement

The stress of the job can create blind spots. You focus so much on preparing your team for Saturday or building next season's recruiting class, that you don't realize you've pushed your **own** financial planning to the side.

And when burnout peaks, we often make short-term decisions to relieve stress—**not** to build long-term security. That's a recipe for regret.

Coaching Pressure + Life Pressure = Financial Fog

It's not just the job that wears on you. Life happens, too. Maybe you're navigating:

- A sick parent or a strained marriage
- Parenting stress with young kids or college tuition on the horizon
- The pressure to be the family's breadwinner
- Career uncertainty—am I getting that extension? Will I get fired?

All of these pressures converge and create **financial fog**—a state where you feel too overwhelmed to deal with money clearly. So you delay, avoid, or go with what "feels good" instead of what makes sense.

How the Brain Reacts Under Pressure

Your brain under stress operates differently. When you're burned out, your **prefrontal cortex** (which handles logic, planning, and decision-making) is overrun by the **amygdala** (which controls emotion and survival instincts).

Translation? You may:

- React instead of plan
- Choose instant gratification over delayed rewards
- Focus on survival instead of growth
- Miss fine print or long-term implications in financial decisions

In other words, when you're mentally and emotionally depleted, you're far more likely to make impulsive choices with money, or avoid decisions altogether.

Real-World Examples of Burnout's Financial Impact

Let's look at a few examples that may sound familiar:

- **Coach A** was so emotionally spent by mid-season stress that he put off contributing to his 403(b) until "after the bowl game." He forgot. A full year of retirement savings—gone.
- **Coach B** was so drained from managing staff drama and recruiting that she ignored her disability insurance paperwork. A knee injury left her out of work for six months—with no income protection.
- **Coach C** accepted a new role at another university with a slightly higher salary—without reading the fine print. Turns out, the retirement plan match was lower, and his healthcare premiums doubled. Net income? Lower than before.

These aren't extreme cases—they're **common**. When the coaching pressure cooker hits full boil, financial clarity is one of the first casualties.

Tools to Reset, Refocus, and Make Smarter Financial Decisions

So how do we fight back? It starts with awareness—and continues with structure. Here are tools and strategies to help you regain clarity when burnout and pressure start creeping in.

1. The 10-Minute Financial Reset Rule

Set aside just 10 minutes once a week to focus on one financial task. That's it. Don't try to solve everything at once.

Examples:

- Log into your retirement account and check your contributions
- Open that unopened email from your insurance rep
- Review one line item from your monthly budget

Rule of Thumb Saying: "You don't need an hour—just 10 good minutes."

2. Use a Monthly "Coach's Timeout"

Treat it like film review. Block 30 minutes each month for personal financial review.

- What changed this month?
- Are you spending more than you planned?
- Any upcoming expenses?
- Any action items from your financial advisor?

Add it to your calendar like a team meeting. Because *you* are the team you'll coach for life.

Rule of Thumb Saying: "If it's not on the calendar, it doesn't get coached."

3. Talk It Out

Burnout thrives in silence. Find one trusted financial advisor, colleague, or mentor you can talk to about money without shame or pressure.

Even just saying: *"I'm feeling behind on my finances"* can help lighten the emotional load and give you room to move forward.

4. Outsource What You Can

If burnout is making it hard to make smart money moves—delegate.

- Use a financial planner to automate investment decisions
- Hire a CPA to handle tax projections
- Ask HR to walk you through your benefits step-by-step

Think of it like a strength coach or offensive coordinator. You don't need to do everything yourself—just make sure you have the right people in place.

Rule of Thumb Saying: "Control the game plan, don't call every play."

5. Protect Your Mind with Physical Boundaries

Fatigue isn't always solved with a nap—it's often solved with **boundaries**.

- Unplug from football after a certain time each night
- Designate one night a week as non-work/family only
- Say "no" to one thing that drains you each month

Mental clarity in your personal life creates space for better money decisions.

6. Track One Number

Burnout makes us feel like everything is out of control. Bring control back by tracking just **one key financial number** each month:

- Net worth
- Retirement balance
- Total debt
- Savings rate

Progress builds confidence—and confidence combats burnout.

7. Visualize the "Why"

Every coach needs a vision for their team. You need one for your financial life too.

- Do you want to retire early?
- Buy a second home?
- Pay off your house?
- Travel with your spouse?
- Fund your kids' college?

Write it down. Stick it in your office. Look at it when the stress hits. It'll remind you why you're making the smart moves—even when the burnout tries to talk you out of it.

Rule of Thumb Saying: "When the season gets long, remember why you started training."

Final Thought: You Coach Everyone Else—Now Coach Yourself

You're constantly coaching athletes to push through mental barriers, stay disciplined, and prepare for the long game. But **you need that same coaching too—especially with your money.**

Burnout doesn't make you weak. It makes you human. And the most powerful thing you can do is **recognize it**, give yourself permission to pause, and re-engage with purpose.

So if you're tired, stressed, or emotionally stretched thin, that's okay. But don't let that moment of burnout lead to a lifetime of financial regret.

Take the timeout. Breathe. Reset. Then come back to the financial game plan with clarity, intention, and strength.

Because when you coach yourself well—you win, even off the field.

Chapter 26: Coaching at Different Levels – D1, D2, D3, JUCO, NAIA, and High School

How Compensation, Benefits, and Financial Strategy Shift Based on Level, Exposure, and Institutional Resources

Not all coaching jobs are created equal—and neither are the financial realities that come with them.

From Power 5 programs to junior colleges and high schools, the **compensation structure, benefits, and long-term financial strategy** for coaches can vary dramatically. Understanding the nuances of each level will help you not only make better decisions for your current role but also **strategically plan for your career and financial future.**

This chapter breaks down the differences, pros, and financial considerations across six major coaching levels: Division I, Division II, Division III, JUCO, NAIA, and High School.

Why This Matters

You can't plan effectively unless you know your landscape. Whether you're moving up, laterally, or even down a level to pursue stability or lifestyle, your financial plan needs to adjust with it.

Let's dig into what makes each level unique—and how to align your money mindset accordingly.

Division I (D1)

The High Exposure, High Pressure League

Compensation:

- Highest average salaries, especially at Power 5 schools
- Top head football/basketball coaches: multi-million dollar deals
- Assistant salaries vary widely (e.g., $45K–$800K+)

Benefits:

- Strong retirement plans (403(b), pension systems, matching)
- Excellent health insurance, travel stipends, relocation packages
- Some offer deferred compensation or annuities

Financial Strategy:

- **Protect your income**: disability, life, umbrella insurance are critical
- Use your higher income to **max out tax-advantaged accounts**
- Build an exit plan—job security can be week-to-week

Rule of Thumb Saying: "Big checks come with big checks on your security plan."

Division II (D2)

Balanced Competition with Moderate Resources

Compensation:

- Head coaches: typically $50K–$150K
- Assistants: often under $50K, some part-time or stipend-based

Benefits:

- Often decent healthcare and retirement, but less robust than D1
- Fewer perks—less travel allowance, smaller staff budgets

Financial Strategy:

- Build a **side hustle** or find summer income (e.g., camps, lessons)
- Prioritize **emergency savings**—unexpected changes can derail budgets
- Get crystal clear on what benefits you actually receive

Rule of Thumb Saying: "At D2, every dollar counts—track them like game film."

Division III (D3)

For the Love of the Game—and a Flexible Career Path

Compensation:

- Lower base salaries (Head coaches: $40K–$90K)
- Many assistants are part-time or volunteer-based

Benefits:

- Varies widely; some schools offer solid retirement and insurance, others minimal
- More flexibility to teach or hold additional roles

Financial Strategy:

- Lean into **dual income streams**: teaching, administration, camps
- Keep housing, transportation, and lifestyle costs low
- Focus on **building long-term wealth slowly and consistently**

Rule of Thumb Saying: "Don't spend D1 dollars on a D3 budget."

Junior College (JUCO)

The Underdog Level with Grit—and Financial Gaps
Compensation:

- Typically among the lowest in college sports
- Many JUCO coaches make under $40K
- Often required to teach or hold other school roles

Benefits:

- Modest retirement plans, usually through state systems
- Healthcare often available but not extensive

Financial Strategy:

- Maximize **state pension systems** if available
- Limit debt and focus on **cash flow planning**
- Look into local housing or cost-of-living programs

Rule of Thumb Saying: "Grind now, grow later—plan like it's overtime."

NAIA

Private-School Vibes with Independent Rules
Compensation:

- Varies greatly: some schools compete with D2, others pay like JUCOs
- Budget size often depends on the sport and school's resources

Benefits:

- Unique benefit packages based on private institution policies

- Some include tuition remission for family members (huge value)

Financial Strategy:

- Investigate **non-salary perks** (housing, meals, tuition deals)
- Focus on **cost-control and side-income**
- Understand contract language—NAIA schools often have flexibility in employment structure

Rule of Thumb Saying: "Cash is king—but perks pay the mortgage."

High School Coaching

Community Impact Meets Financial Tradeoffs

Compensation:

- Varies by state, district, and tenure
- Many coaching roles are **stipends** added to teaching salaries
- Head varsity coaches may earn $3K–$10K+ per season on top of teaching pay

Benefits:

- Strong public school retirement systems (state pensions)
- Excellent health benefits in many districts
- Greater job stability than college counterparts

Financial Strategy:

- Use pension projections in long-term planning
- Supplement with off-season camps, lessons, officiating
- Budget around the **school calendar** (especially for 10-month pay structures)

Rule of Thumb Saying: "Plan like a teacher, hustle like a coach."

Strategic Questions to Ask at Any Level

1. What's my **total compensation**—not just salary?
2. How strong is my **retirement plan**, and am I contributing enough?
3. How secure is this job, and do I have a **financial cushion** if it ends?
4. What benefits do I have access to (health, disability, tuition, housing)?
5. Can I build **side income streams** around this role?
6. What is the **next level**, and how do I prepare for it financially?

Final Whistle: It's Not About the Level—It's About the Plan

No matter what level you coach at, your financial future isn't about your current salary—it's about what you **do** with it.

D1 doesn't guarantee wealth. D3 doesn't mean struggle. High school doesn't limit impact. JUCO doesn't mean you can't invest. **Financial literacy levels the playing field**.

So whether you're calling plays in front of 90,000 fans or breaking down film in a local gym, remember this:

"Your paycheck might vary by level. But your financial mindset? That's elite by choice."

Chapter 27: Exit Strategy – Life After Coaching

P*lanning for Retirement, Business Opportunities, or a Second Career—Whether It's by Choice or by Force*

For every coach, there comes a day when the whistle blows for the last time.

Sometimes you see it coming—other times, it comes without warning. Whether it's retirement, contract non-renewal, burnout, family obligations, or simply wanting a new challenge, **coaching doesn't last forever**.

But what happens next doesn't have to be a mystery. The best coaches have a **game plan**—not just for their team, but for their life after the final season.

This chapter is all about crafting your **exit strategy**—so you're prepared financially, professionally, and emotionally for what's next, on your own terms.

Why You Need an Exit Strategy—Starting Now

Most coaching contracts are year-to-year. Even head coaches with long-term deals can be let go overnight. Assistants can be swept out with regime changes. High school programs shift direction. You may stay in the game for decades, or leave tomorrow.

A coach without a plan is like a quarterback without a pocket—vulnerable.

Rule of Thumb Saying: *"If you don't plan your exit, someone else will."*

Mindset Shift: From Identity to Strategy

One of the hardest parts of leaving coaching is letting go of your identity.

You've likely been known as "Coach" for most of your adult life. Your routine, relationships, and reputation are tied to the game. But when the job ends, that doesn't mean your purpose does.

The key to a successful transition is understanding that coaching is what you did—it's not who you are.

You still have value. You still have influence. You just need a plan to **channel it.**

Part 1: Planning for Retirement

Whether you're 35 or 65, retirement should be a core part of your financial strategy.

Know Your Numbers

- How much do you have saved?
- What will your monthly income look like post-coaching?
- What's your pension payout (if applicable)?
- Do you have investment accounts (403(b), 401(k), IRAs)?
- What age can you access retirement income without penalty?

Consider Lifestyle Costs

- Where do you want to live?
- Will you need to downsize?
- What's your monthly budget without a coaching income?

Create Passive Income Streams

- Real estate rentals
- Dividends and interest from investments
- Consulting or speaking engagements
- Online courses or sports education businesses

Rule of Thumb Saying: *"Your next season is funded by the money you saved in your last one."*

Part 2: Career Pivots and Second Acts

Coaches are natural leaders. You've developed skills in:

- Public speaking
- Strategy and planning
- Conflict resolution
- Team management
- Performance development

Those skills are **highly transferable**.

Potential Career Paths After Coaching:

- **Athletic Administration** (AD, compliance, operations)
- **Teaching or School Leadership**
- **Broadcasting or Sports Media**
- **Business Development or Sales**
- **Consulting for Athletic Programs**
- **Nonprofit or Youth Development Work**
- **Entrepreneurship** (starting your own company or franchise)

Don't wait until coaching ends to explore these. Start **building relation-**

ships, certifications, or experience now.

Part 3: Owning Your Own Business

More coaches are moving into business after their careers. Why? Because:

- You control your schedule
- You leverage your personal brand
- You get paid for your experience and wisdom

Popular business ventures for former coaches:

- Sports camps and training programs
- Speaking and leadership coaching
- NIL education and athlete mentorship
- Real estate or small business ownership

Rule of Thumb Saying: *"You already built a program—now build a business."*

Checklist: Exit Strategy Essentials

Task

Review your current retirement savings and pension projections
Create a post-coaching monthly budget
Identify passions, skills, and interests outside of coaching
Explore possible second careers or entrepreneurial ideas
Meet with a financial advisor to stress-test your exit plan
Consider long-term insurance (life, disability, long-term care)
Network outside of athletics—connect with local business leaders
Secure and review any non-coaching certifications or education
Decide when and how you'll announce your transition (if planned)
Start mentally preparing for a new season of life

Build Your "Bridge Plan"

Sometimes the exit is sudden. You get fired, a program shuts down, or a life event forces change.

That's where your **Bridge Plan** comes in—a short-term plan to keep you financially afloat and emotionally steady while you transition.

Your Bridge Plan Should Include:

- Emergency savings (6–12 months of expenses)
- Side income ideas (e.g., lessons, camps, part-time consulting)
- Contacts you can call for support, leads, or part-time roles
- A short-term health insurance solution if your benefits end

Rule of Thumb Saying: *"Don't wait to build the bridge until the ground crumbles."*

Emotional Preparation: Dealing with the Transition

Leaving the game is emotional. Even if you're ready, the shift in identity can feel like a loss. Here's how to prepare mentally and emotionally:

- Reflect on your coaching journey—what you're proud of
- Stay connected to the sport in healthy ways (volunteering, mentoring)
- Talk to other coaches who've transitioned
- Focus on what's next, not what's behind

This chapter isn't a farewell—it's a **call to evolve**.

Final Whistle: End the Game on Your Terms

The truth is, you won't coach forever.

But with the right strategy, you don't have to fear the exit—you can **own it**.

Whether you're stepping down after a long, fulfilling career or pivoting to something new unexpectedly, your value doesn't end when the job does.

With preparation, perspective, and a clear plan, you'll enter your next chapter with the same confidence you brought to the locker room.

Because legends aren't just made on the field—they're made in how they finish.

"When the play clock runs out, make sure your next move is already in motion."

Chapter 28: Teaching Your Own Kids About Money as a Coach

Using Your Career and Income as Teachable Moments to Model Smart Financial Habits at Home

As coaches, we spend our days teaching discipline, responsibility, and long-term thinking to our players. But one of the most impactful coaching roles you'll ever have isn't on a court or field—it's in your own living room.

Whether you're raising toddlers, teenagers, or young adults, your relationship with money as a coach provides powerful, real-life lessons for your kids. **Your career—its highs, lows, and unpredictability—is a living classroom.** This chapter is about how to turn that into a gift for your children: a financial education that lasts a lifetime.

Why It's So Important to Teach Kids About Money

Financial education isn't widely taught in schools—and even when it is, it often lacks emotional depth or real-world application. That's where you come in. As a coach, you're already an expert in:

- Teaching discipline
- Setting goals
- Explaining cause and effect
- Preparing for the long game

These are all foundational principles of financial literacy.

Rule of Thumb Saying: **"If you coach your kids on money the way you coach your team on game day, they'll win for life."**

The Coach's Advantage: You Live a Teachable Life

Your profession provides *built-in money lessons*—if you're willing to use them.

Unpredictable Income = Budgeting Talk

- Talk to your kids about why you don't always buy the latest tech or take big vacations during off-season.
- Let them see how you plan, save, and prepare for future uncertainty.

Moving for a Job = Planning & Sacrifice

- When you change schools or cities, explain the costs and tradeoffs.
- Teach them about housing decisions, cost of living, and negotiating benefits.

Game Bonuses or Camp Income = Multiple Income Streams

- Use this to explain side hustles, savings goals, or investing extra money.

Contract Non-Renewals = Emergency Planning

- Instead of shielding them, frame it as a real-life example of why you build an emergency fund.

Age-Based Money Lessons

Ages 4–8: "Save, Spend, Share"

- Give them three jars or envelopes labeled for each category.
- Use chore money or allowance to teach basic income allocation.
- Example: "You earned $5 for helping around the house. Let's put $2 in save, $2 in spend, and $1 in share."

Saying: **"Money has a job—give it a goal."**

Ages 9–12: "Let's Budget It Together"

- Involve them in planning a small event or shopping trip.
- Teach the difference between wants vs. needs.
- Talk openly about how you plan meals, groceries, or team travel on a budget.

Saying: **"If you plan your play, you don't lose the game."**

Ages 13–18: "Let's Talk Real Life"

- Openly share how much you make, save, or invest—scaled to their understanding.
- Help them open a checking or savings account.
- Discuss debit vs. credit cards, interest, and compound growth.

Saying: **"Learn the money game before life throws the blitz."**

Ages 18–22: "Let Me Show You the Playbook"

- Introduce them to Roth IRAs, 401(k)s, and insurance.
- Show them your own retirement accounts.
- Talk about student loans, car buying, apartment leases.
- Have them shadow your financial meetings, if appropriate.

Saying: **"If you wouldn't send your players into a game unprepared, don't send your kids into adulthood that way."**

Everyday Conversations = Financial Coaching Moments

You don't need a whiteboard or PowerPoint. Just be intentional. Use normal moments to spark learning:

- Grocery shopping = cost comparisons and coupons
- Family vacation = budgeting and saving for goals
- Holidays = giving, spending, and self-control
- Game check = planning for taxes, saving first
- New job = understanding benefits, negotiating, relocation costs

Let them ask questions. Show them the math. Be transparent when appropriate. Kids remember what they see and hear *more than what they're told.*

Tools & Activities for Coach-Parents

Tool Purpose

Allowance system

Practice earning and managing money

Savings tracker

Visual tool to track progress toward a goal

"Mock Bills" game

Give them fake bills to teach budgeting

Youth bank account

Help them manage money responsibly

Money talk nights

Once a month, talk openly about finances

Savings challenges

Reward them for hitting money goals

What If You've Made Mistakes?

Here's the truth: many coaches didn't grow up with financial education themselves. Maybe you've made money mistakes—debt, overspending, or not saving enough.

Don't let that stop you from teaching. In fact, those experiences make you *more qualified.* Your kids don't need you to be perfect—they need you to be honest and intentional.

Saying: **"If you fumbled the ball, teach them how to hold it tighter."**

Coach Lessons: Your Legacy Is Bigger Than Wins

You're not just shaping wins and losses—you're shaping *generations.*

Financial literacy isn't about making your kids rich. It's about making them:

- **Resilient**
- **Informed**
- **Intentional**
- **Responsible**

Your salary, your benefits, your work-life decisions—they all provide opportunities to lead by example. Every time you plan, save, invest, and budget, you're sending a message:

"Money isn't something to fear or ignore. It's something to manage—with purpose."

Final Whistle: Coach Them at Home Like You Do on the Field

You're already a teacher. You know how to break things down, set goals, correct mistakes, and celebrate progress.

Bring that same energy home.

Your kids may not remember every game you coached—but they'll remember whether you taught them how to handle money, how to set goals, and how to build a future.

Final Saying: **"Raise financially strong kids—and they'll grow into adults who don't fumble the future."**

Chapter 29: Legacy Planning – Giving Back, Endowments, and Philanthropy

Setting Up Charitable Gifts, Coaching Scholarships, or Family Legacy Plans That Reflect Your Values

As a coach, you've spent your life pouring into others—building teams, shaping young lives, and leading by example. But as your career matures, it's natural to start thinking about what kind of lasting impact you want to leave. That's where legacy planning comes in.

Legacy isn't just about wins or titles. It's about what you build that continues to matter after your coaching days are over. It's about the lives you impact, the causes you support, and the values you pass down to your family and community.

This chapter explores how to use your financial resources, career experience, and influence to leave a legacy that reflects who you are and what you stand for—whether through scholarships, charitable giving, or family planning.

What Is Legacy Planning?

Legacy planning is the process of intentionally aligning your financial assets and long-term strategy with your personal values. It ensures that what you've built—financially and professionally—can benefit others for generations to come.

This may include:

- Charitable giving during your lifetime
- Leaving assets to causes or institutions through your will
- Creating scholarships or endowments in your name
- Structuring a family plan that reflects your values

As a coach, you have the opportunity to make an impact that stretches well beyond your coaching career.

Rule of Thumb: "A legacy isn't what you leave behind. It's what you set in motion."

Ways Coaches Can Give Back Financially

Charitable Donations

You can give directly to nonprofits that align with your passions, such as youth sports, education, faith-based missions, or community programs. These can be one-time gifts or recurring monthly contributions that support ongoing needs.

Endowed Scholarships

Setting up a scholarship fund at your alma mater or current school is one of the most meaningful ways to give back. Endowments typically start around $25,000 or more and are designed to generate scholarship dollars annually in perpetuity.

Donor-Advised Funds (DAFs)

A DAF allows you to contribute money now, receive an immediate tax deduction, and distribute the funds to charitable organizations later. It's a great option for coaches who want a structured but flexible approach to giving.

Planned Giving Through Your Will

Leaving a portion of your estate to a cause or school is as simple as adding a few lines to your will. Whether large or small, your gift can make a meaningful impact.

Charitable Trusts

For coaches with larger estates or significant assets, a charitable trust offers tax advantages while allowing you to generate income for yourself or your family, with the remaining funds going to a cause of your choice.

Leaving a Legacy in Athletics

Coaches often want to give back to the game that gave them so much. Fortunately, there are several ways to do that.

Coaching Scholarships

You can create a scholarship for aspiring coaches or sports management students. This is a great way to invest in the next generation of leaders in athletics.

Facility Contributions or Naming Opportunities

Many schools offer opportunities for donors to fund renovations or new facilities in exchange for naming rights. This keeps your name and story alive on the field, in the gym, or in the locker room.

Mentorship Funds

You might fund programs that help former athletes return to school, support leadership development workshops, or sponsor financial literacy education for current student-athletes.

Saying: "Your name on a wall is nice. But your investment in people? That's forever."

Legacy Planning for Your Family

Leaving a legacy also means taking care of your family. It's not just about the money—they need to understand the values behind your financial choices.

Teach Your Values

Involve your children or grandchildren in discussions about giving, saving, and long-term planning. Share what causes matter to you and why. Show them how generosity is part of a well-lived life.

Update Your Estate Plan

If you haven't already, create or review your will. Make sure your assets go where you intend. Include powers of attorney and healthcare directives to protect your family in case something happens to you.

Use Life Insurance for Legacy

Life insurance can be a powerful tool for leaving a financial gift to your loved ones, a charity, or a scholarship fund. It's one of the most efficient ways to create long-term impact with a relatively small investment.

Coach's Legacy Planning Checklist

- Identify the causes, schools, or programs that reflect your values
- Determine how much you can give annually or through your estate
- Explore setting up a scholarship or endowment at your alma mater or current school
- Consult a financial advisor or estate attorney about your giving options
- Involve your family in conversations about your legacy goals
- Create or update your will and legal documents
- Consider donor-advised funds or charitable trusts for larger gifts
- Document your coaching journey as part of your legacy
- Share your story and your "why" with your players and staff
- Celebrate the impact of your giving while you're still here to enjoy it

Final Thoughts: Legacy Is a Choice

You don't need millions of dollars to leave a legacy. What you need is clarity and commitment.

Every coach can give back—whether it's $100 a month to a youth program, a $10,000 scholarship in honor of a mentor, or the life lessons passed down to your own children and players. The point is to be intentional.

Legacy is built over time, with every decision you make to invest in others. It's not about how much you give—it's about the difference you make.

Your impact on the scoreboard may fade. But your investment in people, in purpose, and in the future? That lives forever.

Final Saying: "Legacy isn't built at the end of your career—it's built every day you choose to give back."

Chapter 30: Retiring After 65? Why Medicare Beats COBRA Every Time

As a coach, you've spent your career preparing others for big moments. Game day. Senior night. Signing day. Graduation. But one of the most important transitions—the one most people forget to game-plan for—is your **own retirement.**

If you're retiring at or after age 65, one of the most important decisions you'll make is how to handle your health insurance. And one of the biggest mistakes you can make? Choosing COBRA over Medicare.

Let's break it down.

What Is COBRA?

COBRA is a federal law that allows you to continue your employer-sponsored health insurance after you leave your job—typically for up to 18 months. For many people under 65, COBRA can serve as a temporary bridge to new coverage. But once you hit 65, **the rules change.**

And if you don't know those rules? It could cost you thousands in unpaid medical bills.

The Key Rule: Medicare Is Primary After Age 65

Here's the most important thing you need to know:

> ***If you're eligible for Medicare and choose COBRA instead, COBRA becomes secondary insurance—and in many cases, will not pay for services that Medicare should have covered.***

In plain English: **if you don't enroll in Medicare on time and try to use COBRA instead, you could be stuck paying your medical bills out-of-pocket**—even though you've been paying expensive COBRA premiums.

That's a losing game plan.

Real Example: The Cost of a Missed Enrollment

Let's say you retire at 66. You opt for COBRA because it feels easier—it's the same plan you've always had. But you didn't sign up for Medicare Part B (which covers doctor visits, outpatient care, etc.).

You have a medical emergency. You go to the hospital, see multiple specialists, and walk out with a $10,000 bill.

Your COBRA plan? **It denies the claim.** Why? Because Medicare should've paid first—and you never enrolled.

Now, not only are you stuck with the bill, you may face:

- **Late enrollment penalties** from Medicare
- **Coverage gaps** until you can get back on track
- **Stress and frustration** you don't need during retirement

Medicare: The Smarter Move After 65

If you're retiring or losing active employment coverage at or after 65, here's the smarter play:

1. **Enroll in Medicare Part A and Part B**

- Part A is usually free and covers hospital services
- Part B covers outpatient care and has a monthly premium

1. **Consider a Medicare Supplement (Medigap) or Medicare Advantage Plan**

- These help cover what Medicare doesn't (deductibles, copays, extras)

1. **Add Part D for Prescription Drug Coverage**

- Or choose a Medicare Advantage Plan that includes drug coverage

1. **Only keep COBRA as secondary coverage** *if absolutely necessary*—and only if Medicare is your primary

Common Coaching Mistakes

Here are a few reasons coaches accidentally fall into the COBRA trap:

- "I thought COBRA was the same as my old coverage."
- "Nobody told me I had to sign up for Medicare."
- "The paperwork felt confusing, so I just picked the option I knew."
- "I thought I could delay Medicare and save money."

All understandable. But in this case, a **bad assumption can lead to bad coverage—and worse, uncovered medical bills.**

When Should You Enroll in Medicare?

If you're **already 65** when you retire, you should sign up for Medicare **immediately** when your employer coverage ends.

You generally have a **Special Enrollment Period** (SEP) that lasts **8 months** after you leave your job to sign up for Medicare **without penalty**.

But here's the catch: if you delay, you may be penalized **for life** with higher premiums—and you may have to wait until the next General Enrollment Period to sign up.

Your Post-Retirement Health Insurance Game Plan

Here's what to do if you're retiring after 65:

- **Contact Medicare** a few months before your retirement date
- **Get help comparing Medicare Advantage vs. Medicare Supplement plans**
- **Decline COBRA if you're eligible for Medicare—unless it covers something Medicare doesn't (like dental or vision)**
- **Talk to your HR department or benefits specialist** to confirm your eligibility windows
- **Work with a Medicare planning professional** to avoid costly mistakes

Final Thoughts: Coach Your Own Retirement Like You Coach Others

You've coached athletes through every kind of transition—graduation, transfers, injury, even the pros. Now it's time to **coach yourself** through this one.

Don't let convenience or confusion lead to a costly mistake. COBRA might seem like the easiest option—but once you hit 65, Medicare is the game-winning play.

Make your health coverage decision with the same intentionality you bring to your playbook. Because your legacy matters—and so does your peace of mind.

Part 6: Long-Term Planning and Life After Coaching

Because the Whistle Will Blow—Now What?

No one stays on the sideline forever.

Whether it's your choice or someone else's decision, the truth is that every coaching career comes to an end. The question isn't *if*—it's *when*, and *how prepared* you'll be when that moment comes.

Maybe you'll retire after 30 years with a trophy case full of hardware. Maybe you'll transition into administration, consulting, or entrepreneurship. Or maybe your career ends sooner than expected, because of staff turnover, health concerns, or family needs.

Whatever the case, the smartest thing any coach can do—at any level—is start planning for **what happens next** *while you're still on the job.*

Too many coaches live only in the next season. The next recruiting cycle. The next win. The next job. And that narrow focus can lead to a dangerous blind spot: **the future beyond the field.**

This section is about lifting your eyes from the clipboard and looking at the bigger picture. It's about putting long-term goals in writing, preparing for the transition before it's forced, and building a lifestyle you can enjoy with or without a headset on.

We'll walk through:

- Why your financial planning timeline needs to start *now*, not at retirement age

- How to calculate your long-term needs and define what financial independence really looks like
- The emotional transition from coach to civilian—and how to find new purpose
- Planning for your spouse and family—because coaching impacts more than just your schedule
- How to leverage your network, reputation, and skillset into second-career opportunities
- What it means to retire *to* something—not just *from* something

This isn't just about investing and account balances. It's about **creating options** for the next chapter. Options to walk away on your terms. Options to say yes to the things you're passionate about. Options to keep contributing without chasing the next contract just to pay the bills.

Because coaching might be your identity now, but it's not your *entire* identity. You're more than the game plan. More than the locker room. More than the role.

You've given everything to the game. This part of the book is about giving something back to yourself—**a vision, a roadmap, and a sense of control over what comes next.**

Let's talk about how to transition with dignity, security, and purpose—so that when the final whistle blows, you're not just walking away from something...

You're walking *into* something greater.

Chapter 31: The Power of Compounding – Why Time Is Your Greatest Coaching Asset

As a coach, you understand the value of repetition, discipline, and trusting the process. You've taught athletes that championships aren't won in one game—they're built day by day, practice by practice, season by season. Financial success follows the same principle, and the most powerful financial principle every coach needs to understand is compounding.

Compounding is the process where the money you invest earns returns, and then those returns start to earn returns of their own. Over time, that snowballs into significant growth. It's not magic—it's math, and it's driven by two things: time and consistency.

Think of compounding like building a successful program. Year one is about establishing a foundation. Year two, your team improves. By year three or four, the culture is strong, your players know the system, and the wins start piling up. You're no longer just working hard—you're reaping the benefits of the groundwork you laid early on.

The same is true in financial planning. Small, steady investments grow over time. The earlier you start, the more those investments multiply—even if you stop contributing later.

Let's compare two coaching paths. Coach A starts investing $500 a month at age 30 and does so for 25 years, stopping at age 55. Coach B waits until age 40 but invests $1,000 a month for 15 years until age 55. Both have invested the same total amount, but Coach A's money had more time to grow. In nearly every scenario, Coach A ends up with more in retirement, even with smaller monthly contributions. That's the power of time and compounding.

The problem is, many coaches wait too long to start. They plan to "catch up later," assuming a higher salary or contract extension will fix everything. But compounding doesn't work that way. It rewards those who start early, not just those who start big. Even $100 a month invested consistently in your 30s or 40s can lead to six figures of growth by retirement.

You don't need a high salary or a financial degree to benefit from compounding. You just need to start and stay consistent. Open a retirement account like a Roth IRA or contribute to your 403(b) or 457(b) plan. Choose simple, low-cost investments like index funds, and automate your contributions. Don't panic when markets go down—they recover over time, and staying invested is how you win long term.

Another concept that can help is the Rule of 72. Divide 72 by your average rate of return to estimate how many years it will take your money to double. If your investments grow at 8% per year, your money will double roughly every 9 years. That means the earlier you start, the more doubling periods you experience—and the more wealth you create.

You've likely spent years putting others first—your athletes, your staff, your family. But when it comes to building financial security, compounding requires that you prioritize yourself early. You're not just saving for retirement; you're investing in your future freedom and peace of mind.

Compounding works quietly. You won't see the results overnight, but over time, it becomes undeniable. Coaches who understand this build more than wealth—they build options. They gain the flexibility to step away when they're ready, help family members without financial stress, and create a lasting impact beyond the game.

The sooner you put your money to work, the more it can do for you. And just like with your athletes, the habits you build now shape everything that comes next. So start where you are. Use the resources you have. And give your money the same chance you give your players—to grow, evolve, and reach its full potential.

Let time and discipline do the heavy lifting.

That's how compounding works. And that's how you win off the field.

Chapter 32: Managing Coaching Salaries and Bonuses

As a college coach, your compensation is an essential element of your professional life. Not only is it the reward for your years of hard work, but it also reflects your value within the broader landscape of college sports. Understanding how to negotiate, structure, and manage your salary and bonuses is crucial to ensuring that your financial future is stable, secure, and aligned with your career goals.

In this chapter, we will take a deep dive into the world of coaching salaries, covering salary negotiations, understanding the different compensation structures (base salary, bonuses, incentives), and how to maximize your income based on your performance. Whether you're a seasoned coach or just starting your career, this information will give you the tools and knowledge you need to make smart financial decisions.

1. Salary Negotiations: Understanding Your Worth

Negotiating your salary can be one of the most important aspects of your coaching career. While passion, dedication, and results are essential to success, your compensation should reflect the true value you bring to the table.

Assessing Your Market Value

Before entering a salary negotiation, you need to understand your market value. What are coaches in similar roles, with similar experience and results, earning? Here's how you can gauge your worth:

- **Research Salary Benchmarks:** Websites such as Glassdoor, Payscale, or coaching-specific job boards like CoachJobFinder can provide insight into salary ranges for different coaching roles.
- **Industry Reports:** Look for annual reports or salary surveys conducted by professional organizations such as the American Football Coaches Association (AFCA) or NCAA. These often provide in-depth analysis of salary trends in various sports and coaching levels.
- **Institution Size and Reputation:** The financial capabilities of the school you're working for, its athletic department, and the prestige of the program (i.e., Power 5 versus mid-major) can significantly impact compensation. A coach at a high-profile school will typically command a higher salary compared to someone at a smaller, lesser-known program.
- **Program Performance:** Your team's performance directly affects your salary potential. A coach with a consistently winning program, NCAA tournament appearances, or championship victories is in a stronger position to negotiate for higher pay.

Negotiating Your Compensation

Once you understand your value, it's time to negotiate. Here are some key strategies to follow:

- **Be Prepared:** Know what you're asking for. Go into the meeting with data, industry reports, and examples of your accomplishments. Be clear on your base salary request and any additional bonuses or incentives you'd like to negotiate.
- **Leverage Achievements:** Highlight your career accomplishments, including wins, championships, player development, and any academic or personal achievements that reflect positively on your program.
- **Negotiate Up Front:** If you're negotiating a new contract or an extension, make sure salary, bonus structures, and perks are clearly

outlined from the outset. Don't wait until you're in a difficult position to ask for what you're worth.
- **Bring Up Perks and Benefits:** Compensation doesn't just come in the form of salary. Be sure to include benefits such as health insurance, retirement contributions, and performance-based incentives.

2. Compensation Structures: Base Salary vs. Bonuses and Incentives

In the world of coaching, compensation isn't just about the base salary—it also involves additional components that can dramatically increase your overall income. Understanding these different structures is critical to maximizing your earnings.

Base Salary: The Foundation of Your Compensation

The base salary is the guaranteed portion of your income. This is the amount you'll earn regardless of team performance or other factors. Base salary tends to vary based on the level of coaching (e.g., assistant coach vs. head coach), the institution, and the sport.

- **Assistant Coaches:** Generally, assistant coaches earn lower base salaries compared to head coaches. However, assistant coaching roles often offer pathways to higher-paying positions within the same program or across institutions.
- **Head Coaches:** The base salary for head coaches at large programs can range from hundreds of thousands to several million dollars, particularly at the highest levels (e.g., Power 5 schools). Smaller programs tend to offer more modest salaries but may make up for it with incentives, relocation packages, and additional benefits.

A few things to consider with base salary:

- **Longevity:** Your salary may increase as you gain experience or have continued success. However, make sure your contract includes annual raises or cost-of-living adjustments to ensure that inflation doesn't erode your earnings.

- **Salary Comparisons:** If you're being offered a position, compare your base salary with the market average. Ensure that the amount aligns with your experience and the program's size.

Bonuses: Performance-Based Pay

Bonuses are often an integral part of a coach's total compensation. Bonuses are generally tied to specific performance metrics such as team success, player development, academic achievement, and attendance at games or events.

There are two primary types of bonuses for coaches:

1. **Win-Based Bonuses:** These are some of the most common types of bonuses in sports. A coach may receive a bonus for each game won, a specific win milestone (e.g., 10 wins in a season), or for advancing to a tournament or playoff.

- **Example:** A football coach might receive a $10,000 bonus for making it to a bowl game or $50,000 for winning the conference championship.

1. **Player/Team Performance Bonuses:** These bonuses are based on the success of the athletes or team. For example, a coach might receive a bonus if one of their players wins an individual award (e.g., Player of the Year) or if the team reaches a specific ranking or performance threshold.

- **Example:** A basketball coach could receive a $20,000 bonus if the team qualifies for the NCAA tournament or wins a certain number of games.
- **Bonus Terms and Conditions:** Always pay close attention to the terms that govern these bonuses. Are they realistically achievable based on your team's performance? Are there any restrictions or caps placed on how much you can earn from bonuses?

Incentives: Long-Term Earnings Linked to Program Success

Incentives are often used in coaching contracts to align a coach's personal goals with the long-term goals of the program. These typically include long-term success metrics such as career wins, recruiting success, and tournament appearances.

- **Example:** A head coach may have a clause in their contract that rewards them with a $250,000 bonus if they reach 100 wins in five years, or if their team maintains a high graduation rate for players.

Incentives can be powerful motivators, but they also add complexity. Always review your contract to ensure that the incentives align with what is realistically achievable and whether the goals are within your control.

3. Maximizing Income Based on Performance

One of the most powerful ways to maximize your income as a coach is to leverage performance-based compensation structures. The more successful you are, the more you can earn through bonuses and incentives. Here are some strategies for maximizing your earnings:

1. Set Clear Performance Goals

Before signing your contract, ensure that your compensation is tied to realistic but meaningful performance goals. This includes:

- **Team Success:** Ensure that bonuses are tied to postseason appearances, tournament rankings, and win-loss records.
- **Player Development:** Consider negotiating bonuses based on player success, such as individual achievements like All-American selections or draft picks.
- **Academic Achievements:** Bonuses for maintaining high graduation rates or academic success can incentivize you to support your players' success off the field.

2. Take Advantage of Milestone Achievements

Make sure your contract rewards you for major career milestones, such as:

- **Career wins or losses**
- **Recruiting classes**
- **Conference championships**
- **National titles**

By identifying and negotiating for these milestones, you ensure that your financial success is tied to your performance and achievements within your coaching career.

3. Build Your Brand Beyond the Court

While wins and championships are central to earning bonuses and incentives, don't overlook the opportunity to **build your brand** outside of the field:

- **Engage with media:** Get involved in interviews, podcasts, and sports commentary.
- **Create a personal brand:** Establish a presence on social media platforms, and work with sponsors.
- **Collaborate with athletes:** Work with players to develop social media content, merchandising, and training programs that promote both the program and your personal brand.

4. Stay Transparent With Your Employer

Regularly check in with your athletic department and administration to assess whether your goals are still aligned with the program's needs. This will also help ensure that your compensation remains in line with your contribution and the value you bring.

4. Tax Implications of Salary and Bonus Payments

Understanding the tax implications of your salary and bonuses is critical to managing your coaching finances.

- **Federal and State Taxes:** Coaching salaries and bonuses are subject to both federal and state taxes. Make sure you understand your state's tax rate and how it affects your earnings.
- **Tax Deductions for Coaches:** Depending on your employment status, you may be eligible for certain deductions, including:
- **Travel expenses** (if not covered by your employer)
- **Home office expenses**
- **Professional development and training costs**
- **Withholding Taxes on Bonuses:** Bonuses are typically taxed at a higher rate than regular income. It's essential to plan for this when calculating your total take-home pay.

Pro Tip:

Work with a tax professional who specializes in sports professionals and understands the nuances of coaching contracts, to maximize your income and minimize your tax burden.

5. Future Considerations: Retirement Planning and Benefits

As you focus on increasing your salary and maximizing your bonuses, it's important to think about your long-term financial stability as well.

Retirement Accounts:

Most coaching positions offer retirement plans such as 401(k)s or 403(b)s. Take full advantage of any employer matching programs, and start contributing as early as possible.

Healthcare and Benefits:

Many coaching contracts come with additional benefits such as healthcare and life insurance. Be sure to review these benefits and consider adding additional coverage if necessary. Health benefits are particularly important as coaches often work long hours under stressful conditions.

Final Thoughts: Planning for Success

Coaching is a dynamic, fast-paced career that offers exciting opportunities, but it also comes with financial complexities. By understanding how coaching salaries, bonuses, and incentives work, and by taking an active role in negotiating and managing your compensation, you can ensure a financially secure future for both you and your family.

Remember: success in coaching is about more than just game outcomes. It's about setting yourself up for a career that provides not only professional satisfaction but also financial stability. By leveraging your performance and understanding your compensation structure, you can make your coaching career a long-term financial success.

Let your performance on the field drive your compensation off the field—and make sure to plan ahead for every milestone along the way.

Chapter 33: Saving for Retirement – Beyond Traditional Plans

As a college coach, retirement can sometimes feel like a distant thought. You're busy with recruiting, team performance, and preparing for the next season—thinking long-term may not be top of mind. However, the earlier you start saving for retirement, the more you can ensure a secure financial future, no matter how many seasons you coach.

While traditional retirement plans like 401(k)s and 403(b)s are common, they're not the only options available to you. In this chapter, we'll explore other retirement strategies that can work for coaches, including **deferred compensation**, **annuities**, and **personal investment strategies** that can help you build wealth and prepare for life after coaching.

The Basics of Traditional Retirement Plans

Before diving into alternative options, it's important to understand the basics of traditional retirement accounts, as these are often a starting point for most coaches.

401(k) or 403(b) Plans

Most coaches, especially those employed at larger institutions, have access to employer-sponsored retirement plans like **401(k)** (for private institutions) or **403(b)** (for nonprofit schools). These plans allow you to contribute pre-tax income into an account that grows tax-deferred until retirement.

- **Employer Matching:** Many institutions offer a matching contribution, which can boost your retirement savings significantly.
- **Contribution Limits:** In 2023, you can contribute up to $22,500 to a 401(k) or 403(b) account, with an additional catch-up contribution of $7,500 if you are over 50.

While these accounts are a great foundation for retirement, there are limitations in terms of contribution limits and investment choices. That's why it's worth exploring other avenues to supplement your retirement savings.

1. Deferred Compensation: A High-Earning Coach's Retirement Strategy

If you're a head coach or an established coach with significant earning power, **deferred compensation** is an attractive retirement option. This strategy allows you to delay receiving part of your income until a future date, typically in retirement. It's particularly useful for coaches who expect their earnings to significantly decrease after they retire or who want to reduce their taxable income during their high-earning years.

How Deferred Compensation Works

With deferred compensation, you and your employer agree to defer a portion of your salary or bonuses. These funds are typically invested in a range of options, and you won't pay taxes on the deferred income until you start receiving payments in the future—usually when you're retired and in a lower tax bracket.

- **Example:** If you have a $500,000 salary and a $100,000 bonus, you might agree to defer 25% of your bonus to be paid out in five years. This means you receive $25,000 now and $75,000 later.
- **Tax Benefits:** The income you defer isn't subject to current income taxes, so you reduce your taxable income for the year and defer taxes until you begin to receive it later in life.

Deferred compensation plans can be an excellent way to manage your cash flow during high-income years and supplement your retirement savings. However, it's important to understand that these plans are **not insured** by the federal government and could be at risk if the institution faces financial trouble.

2. Annuities: Creating a Predictable Income Stream

An **annuity** is a financial product that provides a steady stream of income for a specified period, often for life. For coaches, an annuity can be an excellent tool to create predictable retirement income, particularly if you prefer a low-risk strategy for managing your retirement savings.

Types of Annuities

There are different types of annuities, but the two most relevant for retirement are **fixed annuities** and **variable annuities**:

- **Fixed Annuities:** These offer a guaranteed income stream, providing stability and peace of mind, particularly if you're risk-averse. You invest a lump sum or make regular contributions, and the insurer guarantees a set return.
- **Example:** You invest $100,000 into a fixed annuity and, in return, receive $5,000 a year for life.
- **Variable Annuities:** These are tied to the performance of underlying investments like stocks and bonds. While variable annuities come with more risk, they offer the potential for higher returns.
- **Example:** You invest $100,000, and the annuity grows based on market performance, but you also bear the risk of market downturns.

Annuities are particularly useful for creating a **guaranteed income stream** in retirement. However, be mindful of the **fees** that can accompany annuities, as well as the **lack of flexibility** in the payout once you begin taking income.

3. Personal Investment Strategies: Growing Wealth Independently

While retirement accounts, deferred compensation, and annuities are excellent tools, they may not be enough for a coach to build a truly secure financial future. You must also consider **personal investment strategies** that can generate wealth over time.

Building a Diverse Investment Portfolio

A diverse portfolio of stocks, bonds, and other assets can generate passive income and capital gains, which complement your retirement savings. Here's how to start building your own investment strategy:

- **Start Early:** The earlier you begin investing, the more time your money has to grow. Compounding returns can work wonders, but you need time for it to take effect.
- **Asset Allocation:** Spread your investments across different asset classes, such as stocks (equities), bonds (fixed income), and alternative assets (real estate, commodities). This minimizes risk while optimizing long-term returns.
- **Risk Tolerance:** As a coach, your income may fluctuate, and your job security isn't always guaranteed. Consider your **risk tolerance** carefully. In your 30s and 40s, you can afford to take more risk, but in your 50s, you should start to **decrease risk exposure** as retirement approaches.

Tax-Advantaged Investment Accounts

In addition to 401(k) plans, there are other accounts that can help you save for retirement while reducing your tax burden:

- **Roth IRA:** This account allows you to contribute after-tax money, but in return, your investments grow tax-free, and withdrawals are also tax-free in retirement. Roth IRAs are especially beneficial for those who anticipate being in a higher tax bracket in retirement.
- **Traditional IRA:** Contributions are tax-deductible, but you'll pay taxes

on withdrawals during retirement. Traditional IRAs are suitable for coaches looking to lower their tax bill in the short term.

- **Brokerage Accounts:** These are taxable accounts that don't have contribution limits or restrictions on withdrawals. While they don't offer tax advantages like IRAs, they give you flexibility and more control over your investments.

Real Estate Investments

Real estate can provide a steady income stream and increase your wealth through appreciation. Rental properties, for example, generate passive income, while properties that appreciate in value can be sold for a profit.

- **Example:** A coach invests in a rental property for $200,000. Over 10 years, the property appreciates to $300,000, and the coach earns $15,000 per year in rental income. When sold, the coach earns a $100,000 capital gain.

Real estate can provide consistent, long-term wealth, but it requires upfront capital and involves management responsibilities unless you hire a property manager.

4. Understanding Retirement Planning with Multiple Streams of Income

For most coaches, relying solely on salary and traditional retirement accounts isn't enough. To truly maximize retirement wealth, you need **multiple streams of income**. This can include:

- **Side Gigs or Consulting:** As a coach, you have a wealth of knowledge that can be monetized through side gigs, such as personal coaching, camps, or consulting for other teams or organizations.
- **Online Presence and Branding:** Coaches can also build brands that generate income outside of direct coaching. Consider leveraging social

media, YouTube, or publishing books to share your knowledge and experiences. These can provide supplementary income, which helps build your retirement fund.

- **Entrepreneurship:** Coaches can also look into starting their own businesses, such as a sports facility, training programs, or sports merchandise lines. A well-run business can generate income for decades, giving you a significant income boost in retirement.

5. When to Start Planning for Retirement

As a coach, you are typically in a high-earning position during your peak years, which means **time is on your side**. Starting early gives you more time to build wealth, and every year you delay can cost you.

- **In Your 20s and 30s:** Start saving in 401(k)s or IRAs and build a base of investments. Keep expenses low and focus on long-term growth.
- **In Your 40s and 50s:** As you move through your career, focus on increasing your savings and transitioning to more conservative investments. Maximize contributions to retirement accounts, and start thinking about how to generate passive income (real estate, side gigs, etc.).
- **In Your 60s and Beyond:** Begin transitioning your portfolio toward more secure, income-generating assets like bonds and dividend-paying stocks. Think about your withdrawal strategy and how to make your wealth last through retirement.

Final Thoughts: Long-Term Financial Health for Coaches

Retirement planning doesn't happen overnight. It takes careful planning, disciplined saving, and diversified investing. As a coach, you face unique challenges and opportunities in managing your income, but with the right strategies, you can ensure a financially secure retirement.

By taking full advantage of deferred compensation, annuities, and personal investments, and by building multiple streams of income, you'll be better positioned for long-term wealth and financial stability. The goal is to transition from the high-octane world of coaching into a retirement where you're not worried about finances.

Plan today for the future you want tomorrow. Because, in the end, it's not just about coaching your team to success—it's about coaching your financial future for long-term, sustainable wealth.

Chapter 34: Financial Planning for Coaches with Families

Coaching is a demanding profession—long hours, travel, game days, recruiting, and all the pressures that come with leading a team. But for many coaches, the most important responsibility is not just managing a team of athletes, but also supporting a family. Balancing a career that often requires constant mobility with the need to provide financial stability for your spouse, children, and other dependents can be complex and overwhelming.

This chapter is designed to help coaches with families navigate the intricacies of financial planning while balancing the demands of both their professional and personal lives. We'll cover the key financial considerations you need to address when supporting a family, including planning for your spouse's needs, children's education, saving for future goals, and striking a healthy work-life balance.

1. Financial Considerations When Supporting a Family

Supporting a family on a coach's salary involves more than just meeting immediate expenses; it's about ensuring long-term financial security and planning for the future. Here's how to structure your finances to provide stability while managing the fluctuating nature of coaching salaries and bonuses.

Understanding Your Family's Financial Needs

The first step in financial planning for coaches with families is understanding your household's financial needs. You need to think about your current lifestyle and also plan for unexpected situations such as medical emergencies, job loss, or fluctuations in salary (such as off-seasons or periods between contracts).

- **Daily Expenses:** These include housing, utilities, food, transportation, and childcare. If you have a spouse who works, their income may help to cover some of these, but you should ensure that both incomes are aligned with your overall family budget.
- **Health and Insurance:** Medical expenses can be significant, especially if you or your family members are dealing with health issues. Review your health insurance plan and make sure it covers not only your immediate needs but also potential future medical costs.
- **Emergency Savings:** Set aside at least 3–6 months of living expenses in an easily accessible account. This cushion can help you weather periods of reduced income or unexpected expenses.

Building a Family Budget

Creating a family budget is essential for managing finances as a coach with dependents. A clear, detailed budget helps ensure that you're not living paycheck-to-paycheck and that you can set aside money for future goals. Consider these tips for effective budgeting:

- **Track Income and Expenses:** Document all sources of income (salary, bonuses, side income, etc.) and list out all monthly expenses. Don't forget occasional expenses like birthdays, holidays, vacations, or sports-related costs for your kids.
- **Divide Your Budget into Categories:** Make sure you have a section for savings, daily expenses, debt repayment, and discretionary spending. Prioritize your savings and emergency fund.
- **Cut Non-Essential Expenses:** Look for areas where you can reduce spending, such as eating out less or limiting impulse purchases. Allo-

cating more toward savings can build a buffer against unpredictable months.

2. Saving for Children's Education

Education costs can be one of the largest financial burdens for families, especially as children approach college age. As a coach, you may not have the luxury of having a fixed salary every month, but you can still make a strategic plan to save for your children's education.

Setting Up a 529 Plan

A **529 plan** is a tax-advantaged savings plan designed to help families save for future education costs. The best part about a 529 plan is that the funds grow tax-deferred, and withdrawals are tax-free if used for qualified education expenses.

- **Advantages:** 529 plans offer flexible investment options, and some states even offer tax deductions for contributions. This can be especially helpful if you anticipate that your children will attend out-of-state schools.
- **Contribution Limits:** Most 529 plans have very high contribution limits, which allows for significant long-term savings.
- **Naming Beneficiaries:** You can set up a 529 plan for each child, and the money can be used for any future education-related expenses, including tuition, fees, books, and even room and board.

Other College Savings Options

Aside from 529 plans, there are other savings vehicles you can consider:

- **Coverdell Education Savings Account (ESA):** While the contribution limits are lower than 529 plans, the ESA allows for a wider range of investment choices. However, it comes with stricter income limits.
- **Custodial Accounts (UGMA/UTMA):** These are accounts where you can set aside money for your child's future, including education.

However, these accounts don't provide the same tax advantages as a 529 or ESA, and they count as the child's assets when applying for financial aid.

Balancing College Savings and Retirement

While saving for your children's education is important, you also need to prioritize your retirement savings. One of the most common mistakes parents make is putting all their savings into a child's education and neglecting their own retirement. The truth is, your kids can borrow for college, but you can't borrow for retirement. Be sure to strike a balance between saving for college and contributing to retirement accounts like your 401(k), IRA, or other retirement vehicles.

3. Managing Debt: Mortgages, Loans, and Credit

Managing debt is a key part of maintaining financial stability for coaches with families. Whether you have a mortgage, student loans, or credit card debt, understanding how to manage these obligations is crucial.

Mortgage Planning

If you own a home, your mortgage will likely be one of your largest expenses. If your career involves moving frequently, consider renting or purchasing a home with the flexibility to relocate. Additionally, if you plan on staying in a single location for an extended period, you can focus on paying down your mortgage more aggressively.

- **Mortgage Refinancing:** If you have a high-interest rate mortgage, consider refinancing to lower your monthly payments and save on interest over time.
- **Home Equity Loans:** If you're considering taking out a home equity loan for major expenses like home repairs or education, be cautious. Borrowing against your home equity can be risky, particularly if your income fluctuates.

Managing Loans and Credit

Many coaches carry student loans from their own education or from continuing professional development. Balancing these with other family expenses can be tricky, especially if your salary varies. Here are some tips for managing these debts:

- **Refinance High-Interest Loans:** If you have student loans or credit card debt with high interest rates, look into refinancing or consolidating them to lower your payments and save money in the long run.
- **Debt Snowball or Avalanche Method:** Use one of these methods to tackle your debt. The **debt snowball** method involves paying off the smallest debt first, while the **debt avalanche** method prioritizes the highest interest rate debts.
- **Maintain a Healthy Credit Score:** Having good credit is essential for getting favorable loan terms and rates. Always pay your bills on time, keep credit card balances low, and monitor your credit score regularly.

4. Balancing Work-Life Priorities

As a coach, you may have a demanding schedule that leaves little time for family. But work-life balance is important for both your mental health and your family's well-being. It's essential to set boundaries and prioritize your time.

Creating a Work-Life Balance Plan

- **Set Boundaries:** Schedule time for family and stick to it. While coaching requires flexibility, it's important to communicate your availability to your team and institution.
- **Prioritize Family:** Your spouse and children need your attention and support. Set aside time for them—whether it's attending school events, family meals, or vacations.
- **Delegate Responsibilities:** If you're juggling too many tasks at work, delegate responsibilities. Let your assistants or support staff take on

some of the workload, so you have more time for family.

Planning Family Vacations and Time Off

Vacations or time off may seem like a luxury for coaches, but they are essential for maintaining a healthy work-life balance. Plan family vacations around your off-season or during slow periods to allow your family to recharge and reconnect.

5. Saving for Retirement While Supporting a Family

As a coach with a family, one of your top priorities should be saving for retirement while also ensuring your family's financial needs are met. Balancing these goals requires careful planning.

Maximizing Retirement Savings

- **401(k) Contributions:** If your institution offers a 401(k) with matching contributions, maximize your contributions to take full advantage of the match.
- **IRA Contributions:** Consider contributing to an IRA to increase your retirement savings and reduce your tax burden.

Creating a Family Financial Plan

A comprehensive financial plan will help you prioritize savings, debt management, and long-term goals. You can work with a financial advisor to create a plan that aligns with both your career goals and your family's needs.

6. Final Thoughts

Being a coach with a family requires a unique approach to financial planning. By managing your income, saving for your children's education, creating a solid retirement strategy, and balancing work-life priorities, you can ensure your family's financial future is secure.

Coaching is demanding, but with a clear financial strategy, you can balance your professional life with personal goals. Take control of your finances now so you can focus on what matters most—coaching your team and spending time with your family.

Chapter 35: Legal and Tax Implications of Coaching in Multiple States

Coaching across multiple states or jurisdictions is increasingly common in today's sports world. Whether due to relocations, holding multiple coaching positions, or managing off-season training camps and consulting, many coaches find themselves navigating the complexities of state taxes, legal obligations, and insurance coverage in more than one jurisdiction. Understanding how to manage these legal and tax implications is critical to ensuring compliance, protecting your income, and minimizing unnecessary risks.

This chapter will break down how coaching in multiple states affects your taxes, legal obligations, and insurance coverage. With the right planning and knowledge, you can minimize the impact of working across borders and set yourself up for long-term financial and professional success.

1. Coaching Across State Lines: Understanding the Basics

Coaches in the U.S. often find themselves working in multiple states, either due to job transfers or by holding multiple coaching roles across different programs or institutions. This is especially true for those in specialized coaching roles (e.g., assistant coaches, trainers, or guest instructors) who may travel between schools or locations.

When you coach in multiple states, your legal and tax responsibilities change depending on the state laws governing your income, residency, and employment. Here's how these complexities unfold:

State Income Taxes

Unlike federal income tax, which is managed by the IRS and is consistent across the U.S., **state income taxes** vary from state to state. Some states have no state income tax at all, while others, such as California and New York, impose high state income tax rates. Coaching in more than one state could mean you're subject to income taxes in each state where you work, depending on how much time you spend there and the nature of your income.

- **Example:** If you're a coach at a school in Texas (which has no state income tax), but you also run a training camp in Florida (which has a state income tax), your income from the camp in Florida will be subject to Florida's state income tax, despite your Texas residency.

Multiple State Filings and Reciprocity Agreements

If you live in one state and work in another, you may need to file income taxes in both states. However, some states have **reciprocity agreements** that allow you to avoid double taxation, meaning that if you live in a neighboring state with a reciprocal tax agreement, you will only need to pay taxes to your state of residence.

- **Example:** If you live in New Jersey but work in Pennsylvania, you would typically only pay income taxes in New Jersey due to their reciprocal agreement, avoiding paying both Pennsylvania and New Jersey taxes.

State Tax Withholding and Adjustments

When you work in multiple states, you may be subject to different **state withholding rates** for each job or assignment. It's essential to inform your employers about the states in which you're earning income so they can adjust your tax withholdings accordingly. You might need to file additional forms or paperwork to ensure that the appropriate tax rates are applied.

2. Legal Considerations When Coaching in Multiple States

When you coach across multiple jurisdictions, you're not only dealing with state taxes but also varying **state laws** regarding employment, workers' compensation, liability, and insurance coverage. Here are some critical legal considerations:

Employment Laws and Protections

Coaches employed in different states may be subject to varying employment laws regarding:

- **Employment Contracts:** Each state may have its own rules about the duration and terms of employment contracts. For example, one state might allow for employment contracts to be automatically renewed unless terminated by one of the parties, while another state may require explicit agreements to extend contracts.
- **At-Will Employment:** Many coaching contracts, particularly in higher education, are "at-will," meaning the employer can terminate the coach at any time, for any reason, without cause. However, some states have more restrictive termination laws, which can impact your job security depending on where you work.
- **Worker's Compensation Laws:** Worker's compensation laws vary from state to state. If you're injured while coaching or traveling for coaching duties, your eligibility for worker's compensation will depend on the state in which you were injured and whether your employer is required to carry insurance in that state.

NCAA and State Compliance Issues

As a coach, you must ensure that your actions comply with the **NCAA** (if coaching in college sports) and **state regulations** regarding recruitment, training, and compliance with state athletic commissions. Different states may have different **high school athletic associations** or **state regulations for recruitment**, and you'll need to familiarize yourself with the rules in each state where you work.

- **Example:** A coach moving from California to Texas may need to adjust their recruiting strategy to comply with Texas high school sports regulations, which may have different eligibility requirements than those in California.

Cross-State Liability and Litigation

When coaching in multiple states, you need to consider **legal liability**. Laws governing personal injury, negligence, and coaching duties may vary significantly between states. If you are coaching in one state and are sued for injury or negligence, understanding **liability protection** is crucial.

- **Example:** If a player gets injured during a training camp you're running in another state, the laws surrounding personal injury claims in that state could differ from those in your home state. Liability insurance is essential when coaching across state lines to ensure you're properly covered for potential lawsuits.

3. Insurance Implications for Coaches Working in Multiple States

Coaches working in multiple states must be aware of their **insurance coverage**, as policies vary based on state regulations and employment contracts. Coaches typically have access to liability insurance, health insurance, and life insurance through their institutions, but coverage can be affected by the state in which the injury occurs or the coaching activity takes place.

Liability Insurance

Liability insurance protects you in case of legal action for negligence or injury related to your coaching activities. If you are coaching across state lines, it's critical to ensure that your **liability insurance** provides coverage across all states where you coach. Some institutions provide liability insurance for coaches, but it may only cover you while performing duties within the institution's home state.

- **Example:** If you're coaching an offseason camp in another state, confirm that your institution's liability insurance extends coverage outside your home state. If not, you may need to acquire additional coverage.

Workers' Compensation Insurance

If you're injured while performing your coaching duties, **workers' compensation insurance** provides coverage for medical costs and lost wages. Each state has different regulations regarding workers' compensation, so coaches working in multiple states must understand which laws apply to their work.

If your school provides workers' compensation, be sure to clarify whether it extends coverage when you work in other states or participate in camps outside your primary duties. If you run independent camps or have multiple coaching roles in different states, you may need separate workers' compensation insurance for those positions.

Health and Life Insurance

Health insurance coverage is often part of your coaching contract, but the details can differ by state. It's important to make sure your health insurance plan provides coverage in the states where you are working, especially if you travel frequently for games, recruitment, or training.

Additionally, check whether your **life insurance** plan provides adequate coverage for both you and your family. If your family will be moving with you as you take on new positions, you may need to reassess the coverage and policies to ensure that your loved ones are adequately protected in the new state.

4. Managing Taxes and Insurance Across Multiple Jurisdictions

The complexity of managing taxes and insurance coverage across multiple states makes it essential for coaches to maintain careful records, stay informed of their legal rights, and seek professional advice.

Tax Filings in Multiple States

As discussed earlier, you may need to file income taxes in multiple states depending on where you work and earn your income. If you live in one state and coach in another, you'll need to file tax returns in both states and ensure you're not taxed twice on the same income. In some cases, states have tax treaties that allow you to avoid double taxation, but it's essential to track income from each state and ensure you comply with all tax rules.

- **Pro Tip:** Keep detailed records of your income and time spent in each state. If you are coaching in multiple states, you'll need to know how much income is generated in each jurisdiction and for how long you've worked there. This helps in accurately reporting your income and avoiding penalties.

Reviewing Insurance Coverage

When relocating to a new state or coaching across state lines, review your **insurance coverage** for both personal and professional protection. Ensure that your **homeowner's insurance**, **health insurance**, **liability coverage**, and **workers' compensation** policies are aligned with your coaching needs.

- **Pro Tip:** Work with a financial advisor or insurance expert who understands the intricacies of coaching careers. They can help you review your coverage and ensure that you're fully protected in every state you work in.

5. Final Thoughts: Planning for Coaching Across State Lines

Coaching across multiple states can be a rewarding career path, but it does come with complexities. Understanding the legal and tax implications of relocating, earning income in different jurisdictions, and managing insurance is essential for protecting your career, finances, and personal well-being.

To make the most of your coaching career while working across state lines:

- Keep detailed records of your income and work in each state.
- Stay up-to-date on state-specific laws and regulations that affect your profession.
- Work with tax professionals and insurance experts to ensure you're fully covered.
- Plan for future transitions, knowing that coaching careers often involve frequent moves and changes.

By preparing yourself financially and legally, you can navigate the challenges of coaching in multiple states while securing your long-term success and stability.

Chapter 36: Financial Strategies for Coaches with Side Hustles

Coaching is an incredibly rewarding profession, but it doesn't always come with the financial flexibility that many coaches would prefer. Whether it's due to salary constraints, seasonal fluctuations in pay, or a desire to diversify income streams, many coaches turn to side hustles as a way to supplement their earnings and build long-term financial security. From private training to speaking engagements and even brand partnerships, side hustles can help coaches create additional income that not only benefits their present situation but also sets them up for future financial success.

In this chapter, we'll discuss how coaches can effectively manage multiple income streams, balance their side hustles with their primary coaching responsibilities, and invest their side earnings wisely. With a strategic approach, side hustles can become more than just a way to make extra money—they can be a key element in building long-term wealth.

1. Identifying and Building Multiple Income Streams

As a coach, you already possess valuable expertise, a strong network, and unique skills that make you well-suited to develop a variety of income streams. The first step to maximizing your earning potential outside of your coaching salary is to identify the side hustles that align with your expertise and interests.

Popular Side Hustles for Coaches

Here are some of the most common and lucrative side hustles that coaches often pursue:

- **Private Training and Coaching:** Whether it's offering one-on-one sessions with athletes or group training, coaching outside of your regular job can be one of the most profitable side hustles for coaches. This could be focused on skill development, strength training, or mental conditioning.
- **Example:** A basketball coach might offer private shooting lessons or conduct a week-long skills camp during the off-season.
- **Speaking Engagements:** With your experience and insight into coaching, leadership, and motivation, speaking at conferences, schools, and sports organizations can be a powerful side income. This could involve keynote speaking, running workshops, or providing expert commentary.
- **Example:** A football coach could be invited to speak at a leadership summit for aspiring coaches or a sports psychology conference.
- **Online Coaching and Content Creation:** Many coaches are turning to digital platforms to reach athletes and fans. This could involve creating online training programs, offering coaching advice through a subscription model, or monetizing content through platforms like YouTube, Patreon, or social media.
- **Example:** A track coach might create a video series teaching proper sprinting techniques, sell the series online, and provide live coaching through a paid subscription model.
- **Writing and Publishing:** Coaches with a knack for writing can create books, e-books, or blog posts about their coaching philosophy, training tips, or sports insights. These can be monetized through self-publishing platforms like Amazon or through ad revenue from blogs and websites.
- **Example:** A soccer coach could write an e-book about training strategies for youth players and sell it online.
- **Consulting for Other Teams or Programs:** Coaches who have built

a successful program or have specific expertise can offer consulting services to other teams, schools, or sports programs. This could involve curriculum development, program evaluation, or providing mentorship to other coaches.

- **Example:** A baseball coach could offer their expertise to a high school program looking to improve its coaching structure.

Rule of Thumb #1: Choose Side Hustles That Align With Your Strengths and Schedule

It's easy to fall into the trap of chasing every opportunity that comes your way, but when you have a busy coaching schedule, it's important to choose side hustles that complement your strengths and lifestyle. Pick ventures that leverage your expertise while aligning with the hours you have available outside of your primary coaching responsibilities.

2. Balancing Side Hustles with Your Coaching Career

One of the key challenges of managing side hustles as a coach is striking a balance between additional work and your primary coaching duties. Overcommitting can lead to burnout, which not only impacts your ability to coach effectively but can also affect your health and well-being.

Time Management Strategies

To make the most of your side hustles without sacrificing your coaching career, you'll need effective time management strategies. Here are a few tips:

- **Set Clear Boundaries:** Allocate specific days and times for your side hustles, and ensure they don't interfere with your coaching responsibilities. Use tools like calendars and time-blocking techniques to manage your schedule and avoid overlap.
- **Prioritize Tasks:** Identify which side hustles generate the most income or align best with your goals, and prioritize those. Delegate or let go of activities that are time-consuming but don't provide a significant

return on investment.

- **Use Off-Season Time Wisely:** Many side hustles, such as private training or speaking engagements, can be more active during the off-season. Take advantage of your downtime to schedule additional work, but make sure you leave room for rest and recovery.
- **Automate and Delegate:** For side hustles like content creation or digital products, automation tools can help streamline processes. For example, social media scheduling tools (like Buffer or Hootsuite) allow you to plan posts in advance, freeing up time. If your side hustle grows, consider outsourcing tasks like social media management or administrative work to avoid burnout.

Rule of Thumb #2: Create a System for Managing Your Time and Energy

Time management isn't just about keeping a calendar; it's also about managing your energy. Coaching is mentally and physically demanding, so make sure your side hustles are structured in a way that you don't drain your energy. Regularly check in with yourself and assess whether your side work is truly serving your personal and professional goals.

3. Managing Multiple Streams of Income: Organizing Finances

With multiple income streams comes the responsibility of managing and organizing your finances. Whether you're making money through training, speaking engagements, content creation, or consulting, it's essential to keep track of all your earnings and expenses.

Separate Business and Personal Finances

One of the first steps in managing your side hustles is to separate your business finances from your personal finances. Opening a **separate business account** allows you to keep track of all income and expenses related to your side hustle. This simplifies bookkeeping, helps with tax filing, and keeps your personal finances organized.

- **Business Checking Account:** Open a dedicated business checking account where all your side hustle payments go.
- **Credit Card for Business Expenses:** Consider using a separate credit card for business expenses like travel, supplies, or marketing, which can be deducted from your taxable income.

Track Income and Expenses

The key to financial success in side hustles is ensuring you track every dollar that comes in and goes out. For each side hustle, keep accurate records of:

- **Income:** Monitor payments from clients, speaking fees, training fees, and other revenue streams.
- **Expenses:** Track costs associated with your hustle, including marketing, equipment, travel, and software subscriptions.
- **Tax Deductions:** As a coach with side hustles, you may be eligible for tax deductions related to your work. For instance, you can deduct business expenses like:
- Advertising costs (e.g., website, social media ads)
- Equipment and supplies (e.g., sports gear, office supplies)
- Travel expenses related to speaking engagements or consulting
- Home office expenses if you work from home

Tax Planning for Multiple Income Streams

Managing taxes becomes more complex when you have multiple sources of income. Each income stream is taxed differently, so it's important to understand how your side hustles will affect your overall tax burden.

- **Self-Employment Taxes:** If you earn income from your side hustle (e.g., private training or content creation), you'll need to pay **self-employment taxes** in addition to regular income tax. This includes **Social Security** and **Medicare taxes** (15.3% of your net income).
- **Quarterly Tax Payments:** If your side hustle income exceeds a certain

threshold, you may need to make quarterly estimated tax payments to avoid penalties when you file your taxes. It's important to set aside 25-30% of each income stream for taxes.

- **Work with a CPA or Tax Advisor:** A tax professional who understands the complexities of side hustles and self-employment income can help you minimize your tax liability and ensure compliance.

4. Investing Your Side Hustle Earnings

Once you've set up your side hustle and organized your finances, the next step is to think about **long-term wealth building**. Instead of spending your side hustle earnings right away, consider investing those funds to grow your wealth over time.

Build an Investment Strategy

If you're new to investing, it's important to understand that there are different types of investments that can help you grow your wealth. Here's how to approach it:

- **Start with a Retirement Account:** If you haven't already, open an IRA (Traditional or Roth) and contribute regularly. This is a great way to start building your retirement savings, especially with income from side hustles that may not come with a 401(k) or employer-sponsored retirement plan.
- **Diversify Your Investments:** As your side hustle income grows, consider diversifying your investments. A mix of stocks, bonds, and real estate can provide a stable return over time. Many coaches start with low-cost index funds or ETFs that track the market.
- **Emergency Fund:** Before investing, make sure you have a robust **emergency fund** (3-6 months of living expenses) in case unexpected expenses arise. This provides a safety net while you grow your investments.

Reinvest Earnings into Your Side Hustles

Another strategy is to **reinvest** your side hustle income back into your business. This could mean:

- Upgrading equipment or software to improve the quality of your service.
- Investing in marketing or ads to expand your audience.
- Hiring a coach or mentor to improve your skills and expand your reach.

Reinvesting in your side hustle can help you scale and increase future income potential.

5. Final Thoughts: Balancing Success and Sustainability in Your Side Hustles

Side hustles can be incredibly rewarding, both financially and personally, but they also require smart planning, time management, and strategic thinking. By understanding how to manage multiple income streams, balance your side hustles with your coaching responsibilities, and invest wisely, you can create a sustainable path to financial success.

Remember, your side hustle doesn't just need to be a way to earn more money—it should be an opportunity to grow your personal brand, diversify your income, and plan for long-term wealth. With a well-structured approach, your side hustles can enhance both your professional life and your financial future.

Chapter 37: Teaching Financial Literacy to Your Team

As a coach, you have a unique platform to impact the lives of your athletes, both on and off the field. Beyond the physical and mental training required to excel in their sport, there's an often-overlooked aspect of their development—**financial literacy**. Many athletes, especially young ones, face challenges in understanding how to manage their earnings, budget their money, plan for the future, and avoid common financial pitfalls. As a coach, you have the opportunity to teach your athletes how to become financially savvy, empowering them to make informed decisions that will benefit them long after their playing days are over.

In this chapter, we'll explore strategies for coaches to teach financial literacy to their teams, creating a foundation of knowledge that athletes can build upon throughout their careers and into their personal lives. Whether your athletes are preparing to enter the professional ranks or simply want to manage their spending during college, you can equip them with the tools and knowledge they need to thrive financially.

1. The Importance of Financial Literacy for Athletes

Athletes, particularly those who come from humble beginnings or have little financial education at home, are often thrust into the spotlight with the sudden influx of money from scholarships, endorsement deals, and other revenue streams. Without the necessary financial knowledge, they may struggle to manage their newfound wealth responsibly, which can lead to poor financial decisions, debt, and even bankruptcy after their playing careers are over.

Coaches, who are often seen as mentors and role models, are in a prime position to offer guidance and support in this area. The financial decisions athletes make today—how they manage their allowances, their NIL (Name, Image, and Likeness) income, and their long-term savings—will shape their futures. By prioritizing financial literacy, coaches can help athletes make informed choices, avoid common mistakes, and prepare for a life of financial independence.

2. How to Start Teaching Financial Literacy to Your Team

The first step in teaching financial literacy is creating an environment where money matters. Athletes often view their sport as the focus of their life, with finances taking a backseat. As a coach, it's crucial to integrate financial education into your team's culture and make it a priority. Here's how to start:

1. **Make Financial Literacy Part of Team Culture**

- **Introduce Financial Conversations Early:** Start by bringing up financial topics in your team meetings or individual player check-ins. Begin with simple topics like budgeting, saving, and understanding NIL opportunities. Once athletes are comfortable talking about money, you can delve deeper into topics like investments, taxes, and long-term financial planning.
- **Tie Financial Literacy to Team Goals:** Explain how being financially responsible can enhance their athletic performance and career longevity. A financially stable athlete is less likely to be distracted by money-related stress and can focus on improving their performance on the field.
- **Set Expectations for Responsibility:** Just as you expect athletes to take responsibility for their training, discipline, and teamwork,

expect them to take ownership of their finances. Empower them to manage their own budgets, ask questions, and make informed financial decisions.

2. Partner with Financial Professionals

- **Guest Speakers or Workshops:** Consider bringing in financial experts, such as financial advisors, accountants, or even former athletes who have successfully navigated their finances, to speak to your team. These professionals can offer insight into managing money, investing, and preparing for life after sports.
- **Create a Financial Education Program:** Work with your athletic department or local financial organizations to create a curriculum tailored to your athletes. You can structure this program to cover basic financial literacy topics such as budgeting, saving, credit, debt management, taxes, and retirement planning.

3. Key Financial Topics Every Athlete Should Understand

To ensure your athletes leave your program with the necessary financial tools, focus on the following key areas:

1. Budgeting: Living Within Your Means

Budgeting is one of the most important financial skills an athlete can learn. It's easy to spend money quickly, especially when you're suddenly earning more than you've ever had. Teaching athletes how to budget effectively can help them avoid overspending and manage their money responsibly.

- **Track Spending:** Encourage athletes to track their expenses, no matter how small. Apps like Mint or YNAB (You Need a Budget) can help them categorize and understand their spending habits.
- **Live Below Your Means:** Even if athletes are earning large sums of money, it's important to teach them the principle of living below their means. This will help them save for the future and avoid lifestyle

inflation—the tendency to increase spending as income rises.

- **Create a Financial Cushion:** Athletes should be encouraged to set aside a portion of their income for savings and emergencies. Teach them the value of having an emergency fund that covers three to six months of living expenses.

2. Saving and Investing: Building Wealth for the Future

Once your athletes understand budgeting, it's time to teach them about saving and investing for the long term. Without proper guidance, athletes may spend all their earnings in the short term without thinking about their financial future. Helping athletes set up a strong savings plan can lead to financial independence later on.

- **Retirement Accounts:** Introduce athletes to the basics of retirement accounts such as IRAs (Individual Retirement Accounts) or 401(k)s, even if they're still young. The earlier they start saving for retirement, the better.
- **Investing in Assets:** Teach athletes the importance of investing in assets like stocks, bonds, or real estate to grow their wealth. Encourage them to invest in diversified portfolios and avoid the temptation to invest in "get-rich-quick" schemes.
- **Long-Term vs. Short-Term Goals:** Make sure athletes understand the difference between short-term financial needs (buying a car, paying rent) and long-term goals (retirement, home ownership). Teach them how to balance these goals by creating both short-term and long-term savings plans.

3. Understanding NIL Income and Taxes

The rise of NIL deals has provided college athletes with new opportunities to earn money. However, it also presents new challenges, particularly when it comes to taxes and managing income.

- **Tax Obligations:** Many athletes may not realize that NIL income is subject to taxes, just like any other form of income. Teach them about their tax obligations and the importance of setting aside money for taxes. You can also bring in a tax professional to explain how NIL income is taxed at the state and federal levels.

- **Keeping Track of Earnings:** Athletes should be encouraged to keep a detailed record of all NIL earnings, including contracts, payments, and expenses related to their deals. This will make tax filing easier and help them understand their income and deductions.
- **Contracts and Negotiation:** Teach athletes how to read and negotiate contracts. Whether it's a sponsorship deal or a media appearance, understanding the terms of a contract is critical for ensuring they get paid fairly and that the contract aligns with their financial goals.

4. Credit and Debt Management

Managing credit and debt is another crucial aspect of financial literacy. While it's tempting to make large purchases with easy credit, athletes need to understand the long-term consequences of accumulating debt.

- **Building Good Credit:** Encourage athletes to build good credit by making timely payments on credit cards, loans, and other financial obligations. A strong credit score will help them secure favorable terms on mortgages, car loans, and other major purchases in the future.
- **Avoiding Bad Debt:** Teach athletes about the difference between good debt (e.g., student loans or a mortgage) and bad debt (e.g., credit card debt with high interest rates). Help them avoid falling into debt traps by spending responsibly and paying off high-interest debt as quickly as possible.

5. Planning for Life After Sports

Finally, help athletes understand that their playing careers won't last forever, and it's essential to plan for life after sports. Whether they go on to play professionally or transition into another career, financial planning for life after sports is key.

- **Career Transition:** Provide resources or advice on career development outside of sports. Whether it's continuing their education, starting a business, or pursuing a different profession, athletes should understand how to make the most of their skills and interests outside of the game.
- **Retirement Planning:** Even if athletes retire early, they still need a strong retirement plan. Help them start planning for retirement as early as possible, even if they're in their early twenties. The earlier they start saving and investing, the easier it will be to live comfortably in retirement.

4. Creating a Financial Literacy Program for Your Team

As a coach, you can make financial literacy a regular part of your team's development. Here are a few ways to create an ongoing financial literacy program:

1. Host Financial Literacy Workshops

Partner with financial professionals to host workshops on key topics like budgeting, investing, and taxes. Make these workshops interactive and tailored to the specific needs of your athletes.

2. Build a Financial Literacy Curriculum

Consider creating a curriculum or syllabus that focuses on different financial topics each month. This could include topics like understanding credit, saving for college, managing NIL income, or planning for life after sports.

3. Bring in Guest Speakers

Invite guest speakers—such as successful alumni, financial advisors, or former athletes who have managed their finances well—to speak to your team. This gives your athletes real-world insights into how to navigate financial challenges.

Final Thoughts: Empowering Athletes Through Financial Literacy

Financial literacy is an invaluable tool that can empower athletes to take control of their financial futures. By teaching your team how to budget, save, invest, and plan for the future, you're helping them build a strong foundation for long-term success both on and off the field.

As a coach, you have the opportunity to make a significant impact on your athletes' lives by introducing them to financial education early on. Whether you're coaching high school or college athletes, the lessons they learn today can set them up for financial independence and security in the years to come.

By prioritizing financial literacy, you're not just preparing them for sports success—you're preparing them for success in life.

Chapter 38: Financial Lessons from High-Profile Coaches

In the world of sports, high-profile coaches are not only known for their expertise in managing teams, developing players, and achieving victory. They also exhibit remarkable financial acumen that has contributed to their long-term success and security. Whether it's negotiating lucrative contracts, making smart investments, or managing their money during and after their coaching careers, these coaches exemplify the power of financial discipline.

In this chapter, we will explore the financial habits and strategies of successful, high-profile coaches across various sports. These coaches have achieved remarkable financial success, and by examining their approaches to money, savings, investments, and career planning, we can uncover valuable lessons that every coach—whether a head coach, assistant coach, or even aspiring coach—can apply to their own financial journey.

1. The Power of Smart Contract Negotiations

One of the primary financial strategies employed by high-profile coaches is negotiating contracts that maximize both immediate earnings and long-term financial stability. Successful coaches are expert negotiators who understand the value of their work and use that knowledge to secure compensation packages that reflect their worth.

Lesson from Bill Belichick (NFL)

Bill Belichick, the head coach of the New England Patriots, is widely regarded not only as one of the greatest coaches in NFL history but also as a master of contract negotiations. Throughout his career, Belichick has managed to secure contracts that are financially beneficial, while also maintaining flexibility for both himself and the team.

- **Key Strategy: Long-Term, Performance-Based Incentives** Belichick's contract includes significant performance-based incentives, which reward him for team success, making his earnings closely aligned with his coaching effectiveness. This approach ensures that the coach's compensation increases as the team performs better, thus maintaining strong motivation and ensuring financial growth tied directly to his results.
- **What You Can Learn:**
- **Negotiate for Performance-Based Pay:** Like Belichick, ensure that your compensation is tied to team performance and achievement. Performance bonuses and incentives can significantly boost your income without putting your base salary at risk.
- **Be Flexible with Contract Terms:** Having a contract that allows room for negotiation and renegotiation, based on your achievements, can help you earn more over the long run. Always aim to secure clauses that allow for performance incentives, playoff appearances, or other measurable achievements.

Lesson from Nick Saban (NCAA Football)

Nick Saban, the head coach of the Alabama Crimson Tide football team, is another example of a coach who has mastered the art of contract negotiation. Saban's deal includes base salary, signing bonuses, and lucrative performance bonuses for winning national championships, SEC titles, and playoff appearances.

- **Key Strategy: Leverage Public Perception and Marketability** Saban has successfully built his brand and leveraged his marketability as one of the most successful and recognized coaches in college football. His high visibility and success make him a powerful negotiator for lucrative endorsement deals and media appearances, which enhance his earnings outside of his coaching contract.

- **What You Can Learn:**
- **Leverage Your Brand for Extra Income:** Successful coaches like Saban understand the power of their public image. As you build your reputation, seek opportunities for endorsement deals, speaking engagements, and media appearances that complement your coaching career.
- **Negotiate for Full Compensation Packages:** Saban's contracts often include not just base salary but also deferred compensation, retirement funds, and other financial perks. Ensure that your contract includes long-term planning options that ensure your financial future, especially after your coaching career ends.

2. Investing Wisely: Diversifying for Long-Term Wealth

High-profile coaches understand the importance of investing wisely—not just to build wealth during their careers, but to ensure financial security in retirement. Many coaches diversify their portfolios with real estate, stocks, bonds, and even business ventures, building a strong foundation for wealth long after they retire from coaching.

Lesson from Steve Kerr (NBA)

Steve Kerr, the head coach of the Golden State Warriors, is known for his savvy investments and business ventures. Kerr has wisely diversified his income sources beyond coaching, investing in tech startups, real estate, and even media projects. His investments have allowed him to create a financial cushion that supplements his earnings from coaching.

- **Key Strategy: Real Estate and Business Ventures** Kerr has invested in real estate properties, which not only provide passive income but also appreciate over time. Additionally, Kerr's investments in tech startups have positioned him well for long-term financial growth as the technology sector continues to expand.

- **What You Can Learn:**
- **Consider Real Estate and Passive Income Investments:** Real estate is a powerful vehicle for building long-term wealth. Consider investing in rental properties or commercial real estate that can provide steady income and appreciate in value over time.
- **Diversify Beyond Coaching Income:** If you have the financial resources, consider expanding into other investments such as stocks, startups, or even businesses that align with your interests and values. Diversifying your income streams reduces your reliance on coaching alone.

Lesson from Doc Rivers (NBA)

Doc Rivers, former head coach of the Los Angeles Clippers and current head coach of the Philadelphia 76ers, has also made smart investments outside of coaching. Rivers has a background in finance, and he has used his knowledge to grow wealth through strategic investments in the stock market and other asset classes.

- **Key Strategy: Building Wealth Through Knowledge and Experience** Rivers has used his financial literacy to make informed decisions about his investments. His approach is a combination of long-term growth strategies, including stocks and real estate, with an emphasis on learning and adapting to market conditions.
- **What You Can Learn:**
- **Financial Literacy is Key:** Having a good understanding of finance is essential for making sound investment decisions. Take the time to educate yourself about different investment vehicles, such as stocks, bonds, and real estate, and seek the guidance of financial advisors to build a diversified portfolio.
- **Be Patient with Your Investments:** Successful investors like Rivers take a long-term approach to wealth-building. Avoid the temptation to

chase quick returns and focus on steady, consistent growth over time.

3. Planning for Retirement: Ensuring Financial Stability After Coaching

One of the most important financial lessons from high-profile coaches is the importance of planning for retirement. Coaching can be a short-lived career, with many coaches stepping away from the sidelines at a relatively young age. It's crucial to plan ahead to ensure that you have the financial resources to live comfortably after your coaching days are over.

Lesson from Phil Jackson (NBA)

Phil Jackson, one of the most successful NBA coaches of all time, retired with a financial portfolio that included investments in various businesses, including sports teams, and real estate. Jackson's investments allowed him to maintain a comfortable lifestyle even after he stepped away from coaching.

- **Key Strategy: Long-Term Retirement Planning** Jackson's retirement plan was built on long-term investments that would continue to grow after his career ended. He made sure that his investments provided both income and wealth appreciation, ensuring his financial stability in retirement.
- **What You Can Learn:**
- **Maximize Retirement Contributions Early:** Contribute as much as possible to retirement accounts like 401(k)s, IRAs, or other pension plans. The earlier you start saving for retirement, the more you'll benefit from compound interest over time.
- **Develop a Retirement Strategy Outside of Coaching:** Diversify your retirement savings by incorporating investments that generate passive income and appreciate over time, such as real estate, dividend-paying stocks, and annuities.

4. Teaching Financial Responsibility to Your Players

Many high-profile coaches understand the importance of teaching financial literacy not just for themselves, but for their players as well. As a coach, you can use your platform to educate your athletes on managing money, budgeting, saving, and planning for their futures—skills that will serve them well both on and off the court.

Lesson from Gregg Popovich (NBA)

Gregg Popovich, head coach of the San Antonio Spurs, has long been known for his leadership skills, but he's also been an advocate for teaching his players about financial responsibility. Popovich encourages his players to think about their financial futures and has worked with financial experts to help them manage their money and investments.

- **Key Strategy: Financial Education for Players** Popovich provides his players with resources and guidance on managing money, making smart financial decisions, and investing wisely. He recognizes that many players come from backgrounds where financial literacy may not have been a priority, so he makes it a point to offer that education.
- **What You Can Learn:**
- **Use Your Platform to Teach Financial Literacy:** Just as Popovich teaches his players about financial responsibility, coaches can use their platform to educate athletes on money management. This can be through workshops, guest speakers, or one-on-one mentorship.
- **Build Financial Awareness:** Encourage your players to seek out financial education and to develop smart money habits early in their careers. The earlier they start planning for the future, the better their financial outcomes will be.

5. Final Thoughts: Applying the Lessons to Your Own Financial Strategy

The financial habits and strategies of high-profile coaches provide valuable insights for any coach looking to build wealth, plan for the future, and manage multiple streams of income. By learning from their approaches to contract negotiations, investments, retirement planning, and financial education, you can set yourself up for long-term success—both during and after your coaching career.

Key takeaways include:

- **Negotiate for performance-based compensation** and build contracts that reflect your value.
- **Diversify your income streams** through investments, side businesses, or endorsements.
- **Start planning for retirement early** and develop long-term wealth-building strategies.
- **Teach your athletes financial literacy** to ensure they make informed decisions in their own careers.

By incorporating these principles into your own financial strategy, you can not only maximize your earning potential but also secure a stable and prosperous future for yourself and your family.

Chapter 39: Financial Planning During Coaching Contracts – What to Keep in Mind

Coaching contracts are often structured around specific time frames, expectations, and performance goals. Whether you're negotiating a new contract, in the midst of an existing one, or preparing for a potential renewal or termination, it's crucial to make informed financial decisions during the life of your coaching contract. Your income as a coach is not always guaranteed, and unexpected changes, such as contract renewals, terminations, or even market fluctuations, can significantly impact your financial well-being.

In this chapter, we'll break down how to plan financially during your coaching contract's lifecycle. We'll explore strategies for managing your salary, making smart investments, planning for contract renewals, and preparing for potential contract terminations or career transitions. With the right planning, you can navigate the ups and downs of your coaching career while securing your financial future.

1. Understanding the Structure of Coaching Contracts

Before diving into the specifics of financial planning during your coaching contract, it's essential to have a solid understanding of the structure of your contract. Most coaching contracts are negotiated for a set number of years, with the possibility of extensions or renewals based on performance and other factors. Contracts may include base salary, bonuses, incentives, benefits, and other clauses.

Key Elements of a Coaching Contract

- **Base Salary:** This is your guaranteed income, the amount you'll earn no matter what happens during the season.
- **Bonuses and Incentives:** These performance-based payments are tied to achievements such as winning games, making the playoffs, or meeting other program goals.
- **Duration of the Contract:** This specifies how long your employment lasts, whether it's a one-year deal, a multi-year contract, or a rolling extension.
- **Termination Clauses:** Understand the conditions under which your contract can be terminated, either by you or the institution. Many coaching contracts include buyout clauses, which specify how much compensation you'd receive if the contract is terminated early.
- **Renewal Clauses:** Some contracts include automatic renewal provisions, while others require renegotiation at the end of the term. It's important to know how and when your contract can be extended and under what conditions.

Rule of Thumb #1: Always Read the Fine Print

Before signing any contract or agreeing to a renewal, it's essential to fully understand the terms. Working with a sports attorney or agent who specializes in coaching contracts is key to ensuring that you're not caught off guard by unfavorable clauses or hidden stipulations.

2. Planning Financially During Your Contract

Once you have a firm grasp on your contract's structure, the next step is to plan financially for the duration of the agreement. Effective financial planning ensures that you manage your salary, bonuses, and other earnings responsibly, so you're prepared for both the highs and lows of your career.

Living Within Your Means: Budgeting for Coaches

While coaching salaries can be substantial, especially at the higher levels of college and professional sports, it's essential to live within your means. Many coaches experience fluctuations in income due to performance-based bonuses, off-season pay, or the variable nature of coaching contracts. Here's how to manage your income:

- **Create a Monthly Budget:** Track your income, including base salary and anticipated bonuses, and allocate funds for your monthly expenses. Pay attention to both your regular expenses (housing, utilities, food) and occasional expenses (vacations, gifts, or sports camps).
- **Prioritize Savings:** Set aside a portion of your income for long-term savings and emergencies. Ideally, you should save at least 20% of your net income for retirement and emergency purposes.
- **Plan for Tax Season:** If your income fluctuates, it's especially important to set aside money for taxes. Coaches often face tax rates that depend on the size of their income and their state of residence. Consider working with a tax professional who understands the unique tax implications for coaches.

Rule of Thumb #2: Build an Emergency Fund

Given the unpredictable nature of coaching careers, it's crucial to have an emergency fund that can cover at least 6–12 months of living expenses. This ensures that if your contract isn't renewed or you face unexpected circumstances, you can weather the storm without compromising your lifestyle.

3. Preparing for Contract Renewals

At the end of your contract, there may be the possibility of renewal, which could lead to an extension or a renegotiation of terms. Planning ahead for contract renewals is crucial, as it gives you the leverage to negotiate better terms based on your performance, market value, and the evolving needs of your team.

Evaluate Your Performance and Market Value

Before entering renewal negotiations, assess both your performance and the market value of your services:

- **Program Success:** How well has your team performed? Have you met or exceeded expectations in terms of wins, player development, and academic achievements? Use this data to back up your request for a salary increase or extension.
- **Personal Brand:** How strong is your personal brand? Coaches who are well-known in their sport or who have a large following on social media may have more leverage to negotiate higher salaries and better contract terms.
- **Industry Trends:** Stay informed about trends in coaching salaries within your sport. Research how much coaches in similar positions are earning and compare your contract with others in your league or conference.

Negotiating Contract Extensions

When negotiating a contract extension, focus on the following points:

- **Base Salary:** Seek a competitive base salary that reflects your market value, experience, and performance.
- **Bonuses and Incentives:** Ensure that bonuses and performance-based incentives align with both your team's and your own goals. Negotiate for clear, attainable goals that will motivate you to perform while providing a substantial reward.
- **Non-Monetary Benefits:** If salary increases are limited due to budget constraints, consider negotiating for other perks, such as additional vacation time, more flexible working hours, or an improved benefits package.
- **Job Security:** Ensure that the contract includes clauses that offer you job security in the event of an underperforming season or changes in

athletic administration.

Rule of Thumb #3: Document Your Achievements

Before entering into negotiations, gather evidence of your achievements—team success, player growth, personal accomplishments, and contributions to the university or athletic program. These metrics will support your case for a higher salary and additional benefits during the renewal process.

4. Preparing for Contract Termination

Unfortunately, contract terminations are a reality of coaching life. Whether due to underperformance, a change in leadership, or a change in institutional priorities, coaches may find themselves without a job unexpectedly. Preparing financially for this possibility is crucial to ensure that you can handle the transition without significant financial stress.

Understanding Buyout Clauses

Many coaching contracts include **buyout clauses**, which stipulate how much you would be paid if your contract is terminated early. These clauses typically depend on the nature of the termination—whether it's for performance reasons or due to a decision by the school.

- **Review Buyout Terms:** Understand how your buyout will be calculated. Some contracts pay out a percentage of your remaining salary, while others may pay a lump sum. Ensure that you understand when and how the buyout will be paid.
- **Negotiating Buyout Terms:** If you're entering a contract renewal or negotiating an extension, consider negotiating for a favorable buyout clause. A larger buyout can provide financial security if you're ever terminated early.

Preparing for Transition

If your contract isn't renewed or terminated early, here are some financial steps to take:

- **Assess Your Emergency Fund:** Make sure you have enough saved in your emergency fund to cover your living expenses for at least 6–12 months.
- **Seek New Opportunities:** Start looking for new coaching opportunities, both within your sport and outside of it. Keep your network strong, as coaching positions often come up unexpectedly through referrals and personal connections.
- **Leverage Your Brand:** Use your personal brand to market yourself to other teams or programs. A well-known coach can often transition to a new role with relative ease, especially if you've built a strong reputation in your field.

Rule of Thumb #4: Prepare for the Worst, Plan for the Best

While it's important to stay optimistic and focused on your performance, it's equally important to be prepared for the possibility of a job loss. Regularly review your financial situation and ensure that you have a financial buffer in place to ride out a period of unemployment.

5. Final Thoughts: Managing Your Finances During Your Coaching Contract

Managing finances during the life of a coaching contract is all about being proactive and prepared for both the good and the bad. Whether you're negotiating a new contract, planning for a renewal, or preparing for a potential termination, understanding how to structure your income, plan for the future, and protect your wealth will ensure long-term financial security.

Key takeaways include:

- **Understand your contract's structure** and the financial implications of different clauses.
- **Plan for contract renewals** by evaluating your performance and market value.

- **Prepare for potential terminations** by understanding your buyout options and maintaining a strong financial safety net.
- **Be proactive about managing your finances**, budgeting, and saving for both the short-term and long-term.

By taking a strategic, informed approach to your financial planning, you can navigate the ups and downs of your coaching career and build a financially secure future for yourself and your family.

Chapter 40: What Is the Market, the Economy, and Everything Else You See on TV? (Explained with Sports Analogies)

You've probably heard things like:

"The market is crashing!"

"The S&P 500 is on a hot streak!"

"The Fed raised interest rates again!"

"Inflation is out of control!"

It's enough to make you want to change the channel and get back to game film. But here's the thing: once you understand what all this actually means, you'll realize the financial world is a lot like the sports world.

It has teams, strategies, momentum swings, rules, coaches, streaks, injuries, and game plans.

Let's break it down—coach to coach—so you can start building a championship-caliber financial plan.

What Exactly Is the Stock Market?

The stock market is where people buy and sell ownership in companies. Buying a stock means you own a small piece of a company like Apple, Nike, or Amazon.

Coaching Analogy: It's like being part of a sports franchise. You're not just coaching from the sidelines — you've got ownership in the team. When the team wins and grows in value, so does your stake.

What Makes the Market Go Up or Down?

It's all about supply and demand.

If more people want to buy a stock, the price goes up.

If more people want to sell, the price goes down.

What drives those decisions? News headlines, earnings reports, interest rates, political events, even tweets.

Coaching Analogy: Think of it like player hype. A great performance boosts value. A scandal or slump sends it plummeting.

What's the Difference Between the Stock Market and the Economy?

The market is like the scoreboard — it reflects how investors feel about the future.

The economy is the actual game — jobs, production, consumer behavior, and growth.

Coaching Analogy: The stock market is like fantasy sports. The economy is the real game. Sometimes they line up, and sometimes they don't.

Is the Market Risky? Can I Lose All My Money?

Yes, if you invest in just one company, you could lose a lot.

But if you invest in hundreds of companies through index funds or ETFs, your risk drops significantly.

Coaching Analogy: Betting everything on one star player is risky. Building a full team spreads out the risk. One player struggles? The rest can still carry you.

What's the Best Way to Invest?

Keep it simple:

- Use index funds or ETFs that include many companies

- Open a Roth IRA or a brokerage account
- Invest consistently
- Focus on the long game

Coaching Analogy: It's like running your system. You don't need trick plays. Just solid, consistent execution.

When's the Best Time to Start?

Now. Always now. The earlier you start, the more time your money has to grow.

Coaching Analogy: The best players don't wait for playoffs to start training. They put in the work in the offseason. That's how they win when it counts.

What's the S&P 500?

It's a list of the 500 biggest U.S. companies. It's used to track how the overall stock market is doing.

Coaching Analogy: Think of it as the AP Top 25 of the business world. If most of those teams are doing well, the market is strong.

Bull Market vs. Bear Market

A bull market means prices are rising and confidence is high.

A bear market means prices are dropping — usually 20% or more — and people are nervous.

Coaching Analogy: A bull market is a winning streak. A bear market is a slump. You don't panic during either — you adjust and stay focused.

Should I Sell When the Market Drops?

No. Selling during a drop locks in your losses.

Coaching Analogy: You don't bench your starting quarterback after one bad quarter. You stay the course and trust the system.

How Much Money Do I Need to Start?

You can start with $50, $100 — whatever fits your budget. Many platforms let you invest in fractional shares.

Coaching Analogy: You don't have to be a five-star recruit to make an impact. You just need to get on the team and put in your reps.

Can I Make Fast Money?

Maybe — but that's gambling, not investing.

Coaching Analogy: Anyone can hit a half-court shot once. But championships are won with defense, high-percentage shots, and consistent execution.

What's an ETF?

An ETF (Exchange-Traded Fund) is a basket of investments—like stocks or bonds—that you can buy as one single unit.

Coaching Analogy: It's like drafting an entire starting lineup instead of picking just one player. You get balance and depth with one move.

Is Investing Just for the Rich?

Not at all. Anyone can invest — and the sooner, the better.

Coaching Analogy: Great athletes don't all start in the pros. They come from small schools, walk-on roles, and practice squads. Start where you are.

What's the Difference Between Stocks and Bonds?

A stock means you own part of a company.

A bond means you're lending money to a company or the government.

Stocks usually offer higher returns but come with more risk.

Bonds are steadier but grow slower.

Coaching Analogy: Stocks are like your explosive scorers — high upside, high variability.

Bonds are like your veterans — steady, consistent, and dependable.

What's Diversification?

It's spreading your money across different investments so you're not relying on just one to carry you.

Coaching Analogy: You don't build a team with only point guards. You need size, speed, shooting, and defense. Balance wins games.

Why Do People Say 'Buy Low, Sell High'?

Because it's how you profit. But most people panic and do the opposite.

Coaching Analogy: You don't trade your star player during a cold streak. You trust the process and ride it out.

How Do I Know What to Invest In?

Start simple:

- Index funds that track the S&P 500 or total market
- Low-fee ETFs
- Reinvest dividends
- Stay consistent

Coaching Analogy: Don't try to hit home runs every play. Run your offense.

Take high-percentage shots. Play the long game.

What's a Recession?

It's when the economy slows down—fewer jobs, less spending, more caution. Markets may drop, but they usually recover.

Coaching Analogy: It's like a rebuilding year. You don't panic. You use it to train, recruit, and come back stronger next season.

Do I Need a Financial Advisor?

Not to start. But as your money grows, or your situation gets more complex, a financial advisor can be a great coach to have in your corner.

Coaching Analogy: Early on, you run your own practices. But when the stakes rise, you want a strong staff behind you.

What's the #1 Rule of Investing?

Start early. Stay consistent. Don't panic.

Coaching Analogy: The best athletes don't chase every trend. They show up every day, follow the playbook, and trust the process.

What's a Dividend?

It's a payout companies give to shareholders when they earn profits. A little bonus just for owning the stock.

Coaching Analogy: It's like getting extra credit on the bench — you're still on the roster, and you're still getting paid.

How Often Should I Check My Investments?

Once a month. Maybe once a quarter.

Coaching Analogy: Watching the scoreboard every second doesn't help your game. Execute the plan and stay focused.

What's a Stock Split?

When a stock gets expensive, a company might split it to lower the price per share. You'll own more shares, but the total value stays the same.

Coaching Analogy: It's like changing jersey numbers. The uniform looks different, but the player stays the same.

What's a Market Correction?

A 10% drop in the market — it's normal and even healthy.

Coaching Analogy: It's like a timeout after a bad run. You don't throw out the game plan — you adjust, regroup, and get back to it.

Should I Invest During a Down Market?

Yes — that's often the best time. Stocks are "on sale."

Coaching Analogy: You recruit when others are sleeping. Same with investing — smart moves in quiet times lead to big wins later.

Can I Lose All My Money?

If you gamble on one stock, yes. But with diversified funds and smart strategy, that's extremely unlikely.

Coaching Analogy: One player might get injured. But a strong bench keeps your season alive.

Mutual Fund vs. ETF — What's the Difference?

Both bundle lots of stocks or bonds into one investment.

- Mutual funds: trade once a day, often with higher fees
- ETFs: trade all day, usually cheaper and more flexible

Coaching Analogy: Mutual funds are the old-school offense. ETFs are today's fast-paced system — lean, modern, efficient.

Why Do Interest Rates Matter?

Interest rates are the cost of borrowing money. When they rise, loans get more expensive. That slows spending, which can hurt business profits and drop the market.

Coaching Analogy: It's like adding extra conditioning drills to practice. The pace slows down, but the long-term fitness gets better.

What's Dollar-Cost Averaging?

It's investing a fixed amount on a set schedule — like $200/month — regardless of market conditions.

This strategy helps you buy more when prices are low and less when prices are high.

Coaching Analogy: It's showing up to lift, every week, no matter how last game went. That kind of discipline builds results.

Final Thoughts: Learn the Game. Play it Smart. Build Your Legacy.

The market isn't magic. The economy isn't a mystery. It's just a different version of a game you already understand.

- Diversify your portfolio like you build a team.
- Invest consistently like you train in the offseason.
- Don't panic during slumps.
- Stay calm during hype.
- Stick to your system.
- And most of all — play the long game.

Money, like coaching, rewards discipline, preparation, and patience. So put in your reps. Stick to the game plan. And build a financial legacy that lasts far beyond the spotlight.

Chapter 41: What's a Portfolio? Build Your Game Plan, Diversify Your Lineup

Every College Coach Needs a Game Plan

Think of your financial future like a championship season. You wouldn't show up to the court or field without a playbook. You need a strategy. You need defined roles. You need a team that can adjust to every situation and still come out on top.

That's exactly what a portfolio is. It's your financial lineup—a mix of investments that all play different positions. Some are aggressive scorers. Some play it safe. But together, they help you win in the long run.

What Exactly Is a Portfolio?

A portfolio is your game plan in action. It's a combination of different investments working toward your financial goals:

- **Stocks** – your offensive players: fast, high-scoring, but prone to turnovers (risk).
- **Bonds** – your defense: slow and steady, designed to protect your lead.
- **Cash** – your bench: not flashy, but ready to jump in when you need quick access or flexibility.
- **ETFs, mutual funds, real estate** – your utility players: versatile, dependable, and able to fill multiple roles.

You wouldn't play a whole game with five point guards or all centers. Same with your finances—you need a balanced squad.

Diversification: Why You Need a Complete Roster

Imagine putting your season—and your paycheck—on one player. What happens if they get hurt or have an off night? You're toast.

That's what it's like to invest all your money in one stock or asset class.

Diversification spreads your risk across different types of investments. That way, when one part of your portfolio takes a hit, others can carry the load. It's like having depth on your bench. When someone's cold, someone else steps up.

In investing, as in coaching, your best teams are the ones built for the long haul—not just for the highlight reels.

Building Your Team: Conservative, Moderate, or Aggressive?

Your financial "roster" should reflect your goals, risk tolerance, and stage of life. Let's look at the three main portfolio strategies—each with its own strengths and trade-offs.

Conservative Portfolio: Play Defense First

This is the team that slows the game down, controls the pace, and limits risk.

- **Built with:** Mostly bonds and stable assets, a few low-risk stocks.
- **Strategy:** Protect the lead. Don't lose ground. Focus on preserving capital.

Who's it for?

- Coaches nearing retirement
- People who'll need their money soon
- Anyone who values peace of mind over big swings

Pros:

- Less volatility
- Predictable returns
- Easier to sleep at night

Cons:

- Limited growth

- May not beat inflation
- Not ideal for younger investors

Moderate Portfolio: Balanced Attack

Think of this as a well-coached, two-way team—equally focused on scoring and defending.

- **Built with:** A healthy mix of stocks and bonds.
- **Strategy:** Balance risk and reward. Stay flexible.

Who's it for?

- Mid-career coaches
- Those with 5–10 year financial goals
- People who want growth but can't afford to take wild risks

Pros:

- More upside than conservative portfolios
- Handles market swings better
- Suits most investors during their working years

Cons:

- Still carries risk
- Can feel "meh" during bull markets
- Requires discipline and patience

Aggressive Portfolio: Go For the Win

This is your up-tempo, fast-break squad. It's built to score—and it's not afraid to take big shots.

- **Built with:** Mostly stocks, with little or no bonds.
- **Strategy:** Maximize growth. Accept short-term losses for long-term gains.

Who's it for?

- Younger investors (20s–30s)
- Those who don't need the money for 10+ years
- People who can stomach volatility

Pros:

- Highest potential returns
- Great for building wealth early
- Takes full advantage of compounding

Cons:

- Big mood swings (market drops are rough)
- Can tempt panic selling
- Not suitable for short-term goals

When to Attack, When to Pull Back

Great coaches know when to switch it up.

You don't run a full-court press when you're protecting a lead. You don't play a slow-down offense when you're trailing with two minutes left.

Same with investing.

Go Aggressive When:

- You're early in your career
- You don't need the money for 10+ years
- You're focused on growth
- You can ride out market swings

Shift to Conservative When:

- Retirement is within five years
- You're risk-averse or emotionally affected by losses
- You've already built enough wealth and want to protect it
- You need predictable income soon

Your Portfolio = Your Career

Your financial strategy should evolve just like your coaching career.

- **Early Career** – Be aggressive. Build your financial base. Take smart risks.
- **Mid Career** – Shift to balance. Protect your gains, but keep growing.
- **Late Career/Retirement** – Lock it in. Now it's about preservation, not pushing the pace.

You wouldn't keep the same game plan from your first year of coaching into your 25th season. Don't do that with your investments either.

Final Thoughts: Build a Dynasty, Not a One-Hit Wonder

The best coaches don't just win once—they build a legacy.

That's what your portfolio can be. A long-term dynasty. Not just chasing hot stocks or crypto trends, but building something stable, resilient, and real.

Stick to the fundamentals:

- Diversify your investments
- Match your portfolio to your financial "season"
- Adjust your game plan as life evolves
- Think long-term, not just next week

You're not just managing money—you're coaching your financial future.

Play smart. Play for the win.

And when the final buzzer sounds years from now… you won't just have survived the game.

You'll have dominated it.

Chapter 42: Culture, Coaching, and the Money Mindset – The Lens We Don't Talk About Enough

Financial literacy doesn't start with a calculator.

It starts with a mirror.

It starts with your **story**—the one you bring with you into every locker room, every recruiting meeting, every staff huddle, and yes, every financial decision you make.

It starts with how you were raised.

What money meant in your household.

Who had it—and who didn't.

What success looked like—and whether it looked like you.

Before you even opened your first bank account or signed your first contract, your relationship with money had already been shaped by **culture, experience, and exposure.**

Culture Is More Than Background—It's a Financial Blueprint

Let's talk about culture—not as a buzzword, but as a real, living influence.

Your culture might be tied to your **ethnicity**, your **faith**, your **region**, your **family values**, or your **generational experience** with wealth or lack thereof. All of that colors the **lens** through which you see money.

That lens matters.

It affects how you save.

How you spend.

How you invest.

How you talk—or don't talk—about finances with others.

If you were raised to "just be grateful to have a job," you may hesitate to negotiate a contract, even when you've earned it.

If you saw your family go without, you may feel guilty spending money on yourself—even when it's wise.

If you come from a community where financial trust was broken—by systems, banks, even loved ones—you may struggle to believe in planning for the future.

That's not weakness. That's reality.

But once you **recognize your lens**, you can clean it—and learn to see your money, and your future, more clearly.

When You're Not the "Stereotypical" Head Coach

Let's name what doesn't get said enough:

If you're a Black coach in a predominantly white athletic department...

If you're a woman leading in a male-dominated space...

If you're a Latino coach, an Indigenous coach, an Asian American coach, or anyone whose very presence in that head chair disrupts expectations—

There's an extra layer of pressure.

Sometimes unspoken. Sometimes very loud.

You might feel like you have to be **twice as good**, **twice as prepared**, and **twice as polished** just to get the same opportunities.

That pressure doesn't stop at the court or field. It follows you into your **finances**.

Maybe you feel like you can't ask "dumb" questions in financial meetings because you're already being watched.

Maybe you're afraid to admit you don't fully understand your retirement options or your taxes, because it feels like one more strike against you.

Maybe you feel like you have to "show you belong" by buying the car, wearing the suit, staying in the game—and the spending spiral follows.

Let's be clear: that pressure is real.

But it's **not** your financial plan.

The Mental Load of Representation

When you're the "first," the "only," or the "one of few," you carry more than your job title.

You carry the weight of expectation, visibility, and sometimes even **silent scrutiny**.

And often, you're also carrying a community with you.

- You might be helping family financially—parents, siblings, nieces and nephews.
- You might feel responsible for opening doors for others.
- You might be the one everyone calls when they need help or advice.

All of that adds **emotional and financial weight** to your career. It can lead to burnout, guilt, and even resentment if you're not careful.

Here's what you need to know:

Yes, you represent more than yourself—but you still need a plan that prioritizes **you**.

Because when you're strong—financially, emotionally, professionally—you can uplift everyone better and longer.

From Surviving to Thriving – The Shift That Changes Everything

Many underrepresented coaches begin their careers in **survival mode**:

- "Just keep my job."
- "Don't rock the boat."
- "Keep it together, don't ask too many questions."
- "Let me just figure it out as I go."

But you weren't made just to survive.

You were made to **lead**, **grow**, and **build something lasting**.

That starts with acknowledging where you come from without letting it become your ceiling.

If no one in your family ever invested before, *you can be the first.*

If money was always a source of stress growing up, *you can turn it into peace.*

If people look at you and doubt your authority, *you can lead with clarity—and receipts.*

The transition from surviving to thriving doesn't happen overnight.

It starts with small, intentional steps:

- Asking questions, even when it's uncomfortable.
- Sitting with your paycheck and learning how to stretch it, save it, and grow it.
- Saying no to lifestyle pressure and yes to long-term freedom.
- Learning how to build wealth—not for optics, but for **options**.

Your Legacy Is Bigger Than the Job Title

You're more than a coach.

You're a mentor.

A parent.

A spouse.

A change agent.

A living example to every assistant, recruit, and player watching you.

But here's the truth—your legacy won't just be what you did on the sideline.

It will be what you did **behind the scenes**.

Did you invest wisely?

Did you build something for your family?

Did you buy back your time?

Did you create the kind of life that doesn't just *look* good—but *feels* good?

When the whistle blows on your coaching career, will you have something to show for it beyond the highlight reels?

Because the wins that matter most won't show up on your career record.

They'll show up in:

- Your peace of mind
- Your options
- Your independence
- Your ability to say "no" to bad offers
- Your power to retire *on your terms*

Final Word: You Can't Coach the Game Until You Learn the Playbook

You've spent your life studying systems—defensive rotations, offensive sets, player development timelines.

Why not give your **financial life** the same respect?

If you've never been taught how to manage money, that's not your fault.

But now that you've got access to the knowledge, **it's your responsibility.**

So learn the language.

Ask the questions.

Build your plan.

Because the day is coming—whether in 5 years or 25—when you'll hang up the whistle.

And when that day comes, you deserve to walk away from the game with freedom, with peace, and with no regrets.

You're not just a coach.

You're a legacy builder.

Let's get to work.

Chapter 43: When Smart Coaches Make Dumb Money Moves

Coaches are leaders. Thinkers. Competitors. Motivators. Whether you're breaking down film at 2 a.m. or strategizing your next recruiting class, your brain is wired for problem-solving and game planning. But when it comes to money? Even the smartest coaches can fumble the bag.

This chapter is about those fumbles — the investment traps, money schemes, and bad decisions that coaches, despite their intelligence and hard-earned salaries, often fall into. It's not because they're careless. It's because they're overworked, under-advised, and operating under pressure — from peers, from society, and sometimes from their own egos.

We're going to break down the most common financial mistakes college coaches make, why they're so tempting, and how you can avoid them — not just for your money's sake, but for your peace of mind.

Why Coaches Get Caught Slipping

Big Salaries, Little Financial Education

You might be making $150K, $300K, or even more. But nobody ever taught you how to manage a six-figure income. That contract didn't come with a crash course on investing or taxes.

Peer Pressure in the Coaches Circle

If your assistant coach is investing in a "can't miss" opportunity, or the head coach is building a luxury vacation home, it's hard not to feel like you should be doing something big, too.

No Time, No Energy

Long days, travel, recruiting, film sessions — by the time you get home, you don't have the time or brainpower to do deep financial research. So you outsource decisions or act off of gut feelings.

Delayed Gratification Mentality

After years of grinding as a GA, taking low-paying jobs, and hustling your way up the coaching ladder, it's tempting to "reward" yourself too early. You deserve nice things — but reckless investing isn't one of them.

Trying to Flex with the Big Names

Let's be real: in athletics, image matters. You wear the logo, drive the car, stay in the right hotel. And when you're surrounded by boosters, athletes, and alumni with deep pockets, it's easy to play outside your weight class financially.

The Traps Coaches Fall Into

1. The "Exclusive" Private Investment

A former player's dad, an alum, or a fellow coach hits you with an inside opportunity. Maybe it's a new NIL agency, sports tech startup, or something in crypto. They promise high returns, low risk, and fast results.

Red Flags:

- No financials or business plan
- "We're closing the round this week" urgency
- You don't fully understand how it makes money

Reality:

Startups fail all the time. If you didn't scout it properly, you're just gambling. You wouldn't offer a scholarship without seeing game film — don't invest without doing your homework.

2. Real Estate Syndication Confusion

Someone pitches you on a passive real estate deal: "Throw in $50K and get mailbox money every month." Sounds easy, right?

Red Flags:

- Overcomplicated structures
- Vague promises and "guaranteed" returns
- No clarity on what happens if the deal fails

Reality:

These deals can work — if run by pros with a track record. But many are smoke and mirrors, with investors footing the bill for someone else's bad math.

3. Ponzi Schemes Dressed as "Opportunities"

A friend says they're making 3% a month trading crypto or foreign currency. You don't understand it — but it seems like free money. They even show you screenshots.

Red Flags:

- No explanation of how the returns are generated
- Encouraged to "recruit others"
- Returns are steady no matter what the market's doing

Reality:

If it sounds too good to be true, it is. These "opportunities" usually collapse — and you're left explaining to your spouse where the $40K went.

4. The Coach-Owned Bar or Restaurant

You invest in a sports bar near campus. It sounds like fun, your name's on the wall, and it's a great place to hang with boosters.

Red Flags:

- No restaurant experience on the team
- Overestimated profits

- You're emotionally invested in the "vibe" more than the business

Reality:

Restaurants are notoriously risky. It's not just a hangout spot — it's a business. And most fail within a few years.

5. MLMs and Side Hustle Nightmares

Yes, even college coaches get pulled into selling shakes, skincare, or "health tech" through multi-level marketing.

Red Flags:

- You need to buy inventory
- You earn more by recruiting than selling
- You're encouraged to "be your own boss" with no real plan

Reality:

MLMs prey on ambitious people looking for extra income. But most folks lose money — and credibility — chasing the promise.

6. The Next Big Medical/NIL Startup

It's pitched as revolutionary — a new wearable tech, NIL tracking app, or performance-enhancing device. You're told it's the future of sports.

Red Flags:

- No working prototype or proof of concept
- No legal protection or patent
- Based purely on hype

Reality:

A lot of these companies go nowhere. If you wouldn't trust it in your program, don't invest in it.

The Mindset Behind the Mistakes

Overconfidence Bias

You're used to leading. Making quick decisions. That confidence can spill into investing, where slower is better.

Groupthink

Everyone in the coaching office is in the deal, so you feel like you should be, too. But if the whole staff is wrong? Now you're all broke — together.

Anchoring to Income

You make $200K, so $25K doesn't feel like a big deal. Until it disappears.

FOMO

You hear about someone making a killing, and you jump in too late. By the time you hear about the "next big thing," it's already peaked.

Smart Questions to Ask Before Investing

- Do I actually understand how this makes money?
- Is my money locked up? Can I access it if needed?
- Who is managing this — and what's their track record?
- What happens if it fails?
- Am I making this decision emotionally or logically?
- Did I run this by a financial advisor or attorney?
- Would I feel comfortable if this money vanished tomorrow?

Better Alternatives for Coaches

Index Funds

Low-fee, wide exposure to the stock market. No drama, just growth.

Backdoor Roth IRA

Great tax strategy for high earners who want tax-free money later.

Taxable Brokerage Account

Flexible. Invest what you want, when you want. No income limits.

Real Estate — Done Right

Direct ownership or REITs (real estate investment trusts). Know your role — either be the landlord, or hire one.

Paying Off Debt

It's like a guaranteed return. Eliminating a 6% loan is the same as earning 6% risk-free.

Professional Development

Courses, certifications, coaching clinics — the more value you bring, the more money you can command.

Real-Life Coaching Cautionary Tales

Coach T and the Crypto Collapse

Invested $60K in a digital currency app he didn't understand. "It's like Venmo but decentralized." Two months later, the site was gone. So was the money.

Coach L and the Boring Path

Funded a Roth IRA yearly, kept it simple with ETFs, and bought a duplex with help from a trusted advisor. Five years later? $400K net worth and sleeping just fine.

Coach D and the Downtown Lounge

Invested $90K in a "sports lounge" with friends. They said it would be the spot for athletes and fans. It closed before the second basketball season tipped off.

Pitfalls to Watch Out For

- High fees with little explanation
- "Guaranteed" returns
- Being asked to recruit others
- No exit strategy
- Emotional attachment
- Rushed decisions without vetting
- No financial or legal review

How to Shut It Down With Class

People will approach you because you're "Coach." Here's how to respectfully say no:

"Appreciate you thinking of me. I have a policy to only invest after full due diligence and input from my financial team. Wishing you success with your project."

Short. Professional. Done.

Final Thought: Be Boring, Be Wealthy

You don't need to impress anyone with risky investments. You already made it. Your title, your resume, your work ethic — that's the flex.

Real wealth comes from patience, consistency, and avoiding unforced errors. Build your legacy the same way you build your team: with discipline, structure, and smart decisions.

Because while the season might be won in March, your wealth is built in the offseason. Be strategic. Be focused.

And don't let your money make you look foolish — not when you've worked this hard to be this smart.

Chapter 44: Should Coaches Take Financial Advice from Other Coaches?

As a college coach, you're constantly surrounded by other smart, driven professionals — the type of people who thrive under pressure, solve problems on the fly, and lead teams through adversity. In the locker room, at staff dinners, and during long recruiting trips, money talk comes up. "You should check out this real estate deal." "I'm putting money into this sports tech startup." "You still haven't bought crypto?"

It's natural to listen to your coaching peers. They know your lifestyle — the grind, the income jumps, the job insecurity, the tax issues that come with bonuses or camps. And when another coach seems like they're doing well financially, it's easy to think, *"If it worked for them, it could work for me."*

But here's the catch: just because someone is smart, successful, or respected in their profession doesn't mean they're a financial expert. And taking financial advice from other coaches — especially those who don't work with a financial advisor — can be risky business.

In this chapter, we'll break down the benefits and dangers of following money advice from your coaching circle, and we'll give you some rules of thumb to help you make better, more informed decisions.

Why It's Tempting to Take Financial Advice from Other Coaches

Shared Struggles and Lifestyles

Other coaches know what it's like to live on that GA salary, take the low-paying job for a better title, and finally land a six-figure contract after years of hustle. That shared path makes their financial advice feel relevant and relatable.

No Added Cost

Getting tips from a fellow coach over lunch doesn't cost a dime — unlike hiring a financial advisor, which can come with management fees or flat fees. When someone offers free insight, especially if it "worked for them," it feels like a good deal.

Trust in the Relationship

Coaches build strong bonds. You've been in the trenches together. If another coach is sharing a money move, it feels more trustworthy than a cold call from a financial firm or a guy in a suit trying to sell you something.

Real-World Experience

There's something powerful about hearing, "I invested in this condo three years ago and just doubled my money." It's not a textbook or a theory — it's lived experience. And real-life examples feel more concrete than hypothetical financial scenarios.

The Dangers of Taking Money Advice from Coaches Who Don't Use Advisors

1. Smart in Coaching ≠ Smart in Finance

Being a great offensive coordinator doesn't automatically make you good at picking stocks or structuring retirement plans. Many coaches confuse confidence in their leadership with financial literacy — and that overconfidence can lead to bad moves.

Just like you wouldn't trust a financial planner to draw up a goal-line play, you shouldn't take unqualified advice on building wealth just because the person giving it is respected in your profession.

2. Limited Scope and Experience

A fellow coach might tell you about flipping houses, buying crypto, or investing in their brother-in-law's startup. But they may not have a full understanding of risk tolerance, asset allocation, tax implications, or long-term strategy. They might've gotten lucky — or they might not be telling you about their losses.

Coaches tend to talk about their wins, not their L's.

3. Hidden Bias or Conflicts of Interest

That "great" investment opportunity they're hyping? They might be knee-deep in it and need more investors to keep it afloat. Or they could be emotionally invested and want you to validate their decision. Either way, you're not getting objective advice — you're getting someone else's financial echo chamber.

4. The Herd Mentality

If everyone on your staff is investing in something, it's hard not to follow. But groupthink can be dangerous. Just because five people say something's smart doesn't make it true. Remember, it's possible to be in a room full of intelligent people all making the same bad call.

5. Short-Term Thinking

Many coaches live year to year — one bad season and the job might be gone. That pressure can lead to short-term, get-rich-quick thinking. Your peers might focus on "quick flips" or high-risk plays, not a sustainable long-term plan that supports retirement, your family, and future career changes.

Real-Life Coaching Scenarios

Coach B and the Real Estate Hustle

Coach B bought into a real estate deal with three other coaches. They planned to Airbnb it out near a football stadium. After two seasons of no guests, local restrictions, and rising expenses, the property was sold at a loss — and the friendships were never the same.

Coach M and the Quiet Winner

Instead of chasing "hot" deals, Coach M worked with a fiduciary advisor, maxed out his 403(b), invested in low-cost index funds, and saved consistently. Ten years later, he's got peace of mind, minimal stress, and a growing nest egg — without having to guess or gamble.

Rules of Thumb for Navigating Peer Advice

1. Ask What They Know and How They Know It

Before taking advice, ask: *Where did you learn that? How has it worked for you long-term? What's your strategy beyond this one move?* If they can't answer clearly, it's not advice — it's opinion.

2. Don't Confuse Familiarity with Expertise

Just because someone shares your job title doesn't mean they've done the research. Know the difference between "I heard" and "I verified."

3. Get a Second (and Third) Opinion

Before moving money, talk to a certified financial planner, CPA, or even an attorney. Different perspectives help you see blind spots.

4. Customize Your Game Plan

Every coach has different obligations — kids, debt, retirement goals, spouse income, etc. Don't copy-paste someone else's playbook. You need a strategy built around *your* life.

5. Don't Let Ego or Image Drive Your Choices

You don't need to buy a rental property, start a business, or invest in crypto just to impress your staff or peers. Build quietly, build intentionally, and let your portfolio grow — not your persona.

6. Use Advisors Like You Use Coordinators

Even the best head coaches don't call every play. They delegate, they lean on experts. Do the same with your money. A fiduciary advisor helps you build a big-picture plan and keeps your emotions in check.

Final Thought: Be the Coach, Not the Gambler

The best coaches know when to call the shots and when to hand off. Your financial future deserves more than guesswork and locker room tips.

So the next time a fellow coach pitches you on a "sure thing," ask yourself:

- Does this fit into my long-term plan?
- Do I understand the risk?
- Would I take this same advice from a stranger?

Your career is built on preparation, game planning, and discipline. Your finances should be no different.

Don't let peer pressure cost you peace.

Don't let confidence turn into carelessness.

Don't let a coach's hot tip become your cold reality.

Trust the process. Trust the plan. Build wealth the way you built your career — with purpose.

Chapter 45: Conclusion Win the Game of Life, Not Just the Season

Success Isn't Just a Record—It's a Legacy

You've given everything to the game.

The early mornings, the late nights. The long bus rides, the tough conversations, the hard losses and the unforgettable wins. You've built programs, developed young lives, and carried the weight of a thousand expectations.

But here's the truth that often gets overlooked: **coaching success isn't just measured in banners and bowl games—it's measured in what you build for yourself and your family when the crowd goes quiet.**

Because while winning today feels good, **being financially free tomorrow feels even better.**

It's easy to get caught up in the cycle.

The next season. The next recruit. The next job.

But what happens when there is no next?

Did you plan for it?

Did you protect your income, your name, your family?

Did you turn your knowledge into opportunity?

Did you build a future where you could say, *"I'm good—on and off the field"*?

This book wasn't written to overwhelm you with financial jargon. It was written to **give you control**, the same control you demand in the film room, on the practice field, and in your culture.

You already know how to build systems.

You already believe in structure, consistency, and long-term thinking.

Now, apply that same mindset to your finances—**and win the game that really matters.**

Here's what that looks like:

- Budget with intention, not reaction
- Save and invest consistently, not occasionally
- Protect your income with insurance, not hope
- Build a financial team like you build a coaching staff
- Teach your family the same principles you live by
- Make your money work, so you don't have to work forever

Write your own playbook.

Not just for the next job, but for the next 30 years. For your spouse. For your kids. For the future version of you who wants peace more than pressure.

Because at the end of the day, no one looks back and wishes they'd worked more camps or recruited one more athlete.

They wish they'd had **more time, more choices, and more freedom** to live life on their terms.

So coach, take this seriously. Start now. Start where you are.

And just like you've done your whole life—**lead with discipline, purpose, and vision.**

Win the game of life.

Because your greatest victory should come **after** the final whistle.

About the Author

Pat Brown, MBA, is more than a financial advisor—he's a coach at heart.

A former Division I football captain at the University of Kansas and professional athlete with the Calgary Stampeders of the CFL, Pat understands the pressure, unpredictability, and sacrifice that come with the world of athletics. He's walked in those shoes—and now he's using his experience to help others walk a smarter financial path.

With over two decades of experience in financial planning, insurance, and investment management, Pat has advised families, professionals, and athletes at every stage of life. But his mission is deeper than just money—it's about **education, empowerment, and legacy.**

He's the founder of several groundbreaking financial literacy platforms, including:

- **Financial Literacy For NIL**
- **Financial Literacy For Student-Athletes**
- **Financial Literacy For College Coaches**
- **Parents Of Student Athletes**
- **Financial Literacy For Doctors**
- **Financial Literacy For Attorneys**
- **Financial Literacy For Pro Athletes**
- **Financial Literacy For The Culture**

Pat's passion for financial literacy was born from personal experience. As a student-athlete, he didn't grow up with financial education at the dinner table. He saw what a lack of knowledge could cost—not just in dollars, but in opportunity and peace of mind. That drove him to earn his MBA, study the game of money the way he once studied game film, and become the financial advocate he wishes every athlete and coach had.

He's now a sought-after speaker, educator, and advisor who brings real talk and real tools to locker rooms, campuses, churches, and boardrooms across the country.

Pat lives in Kansas with his wife Cassandra, and their daughters are charting their own paths across the country—**Peyton lives in California**, and **Ryan lives in New York.** His love for family drives his passion for legacy-building, and his background as a leader on and off the field shapes his no-nonsense, heart-first approach to financial education.

Whether he's breaking down a budget, helping a coach negotiate a contract, or speaking to a room full of student-athletes about NIL, Pat's mission is clear:

Help people win—not just in the game, but in life.

Disclaimer and Purpose of This Book

Financial Literacy For College Coaches is written with the intent to educate, empower, and encourage college coaches—at all levels—to take control of their financial lives and, in turn, become better guides for the student-athletes they lead. The information shared throughout these pages draws from the author's personal journey, professional experience, and over two decades of work in financial services, athlete development, and educational outreach.

However, it is critical to understand the following:

Educational Use Only

The content of this book is intended solely for educational and informational purposes. It is designed to help college coaches build foundational knowledge in key areas such as budgeting, investing, taxes, insurance, contracts, retirement, and NIL awareness—not to offer customized financial advice.

Coaches are often role models and decision-makers in young athletes' lives. This book seeks to equip them with the tools to make informed choices and ask the right questions, both for their personal lives and in their support of others. That said, this book is not a financial plan. It is not specific to any one reader's personal, legal, or financial circumstances.

Every individual's financial, legal, and professional situation is unique. Before making any important decisions related to money, contracts, benefits, or business ventures, it is strongly advised that you consult with a licensed professional.

No Legal Advice

While this book touches on legal concepts that coaches may encounter—such as employment contracts, NIL guidance, or business formation—it does not offer legal advice. If you are considering signing a personal services contract, launching a side business, negotiating a coaching contract, or advising athletes on legal matters, always consult with an attorney who is licensed in your state and experienced in the relevant field of law.

The laws surrounding NIL, employment, liability, and intellectual property vary widely and are constantly evolving. It is your responsibility to stay compliant with relevant state, institutional, and NCAA regulations, and ensure that any guidance you provide to others is legally sound and up to date.

No Financial or Investment Advice

This book covers a wide range of financial topics—retirement planning, budgeting, insurance, investing, taxes, and more—but it does so from an educational perspective only. It is not intended to provide personalized investment advice or specific financial product recommendations.

You should not act solely on the basis of the information presented here without consulting with a Certified Financial Planner™, fiduciary advisor, or other licensed financial professional. Decisions about money should reflect your unique financial situation, including income, risk tolerance, goals, and responsibilities.

Nothing in this book guarantees investment success or promises specific financial results. Examples used are hypothetical and for illustrative purposes only.

No Tax or Accounting Advice

This book is not written by a CPA, enrolled agent, or licensed tax preparer. Any references to taxes—whether related to NIL income, self-employment, deductions, or IRS compliance—are general in nature and should not be interpreted as tax advice.

As a coach, your income may include bonuses, endorsements, camp revenue, or consulting work—each of which may be taxed differently. The same applies when advising athletes or colleagues who earn income from multiple sources. For proper tax planning, preparation, and compliance, seek advice from a qualified tax professional.

Only a licensed CPA or enrolled agent can help you accurately file, estimate quarterly taxes, and avoid costly penalties.

No Guarantees or Promises

Reading this book does not guarantee financial security, career advancement, or NIL expertise. Your results will depend on multiple factors, including your personal financial habits, the quality of your decision-making, the advice you receive, and sometimes—circumstances beyond your control.

This book is meant to motivate, inspire, and guide—not to predict or promise specific outcomes.

Limitation of Liability

By reading this book, you acknowledge that the author, Pat Brown, MBA, and all associated platforms—including but not limited to FinancialLiteracyForCollegeCoaches.com, FinancialLiteracyForNIL.com, and FinancialLiteracyForStudentAthletes.com—are not responsible for the decisions you make based on the content herein.

Neither the author nor affiliated entities assume any liability for financial loss, legal trouble, tax complications, or personal outcomes that may arise as a result of applying the information provided.

Build a Trusted Team

It is the author's firm belief that every college coach—like every student-athlete—deserves a support system that includes legal, financial, and tax professionals. This book is meant to complement that system, not replace it.

If you do not currently work with a licensed advisor, attorney, or CPA, this is your sign to begin building your financial team now. Whether you're negotiating a new contract, planning for retirement, advising an athlete, or launching a business on the side, having the right professionals in your corner can make all the difference.

You spend your life preparing others for success—make sure you do the same for yourself.

Important Dates for College Coaches

Stay Financially Organized Throughout the Year

JANUARY

January 15 – Quarterly Estimated Tax Payment Due

If you earn side income (camps, speaking, consulting) not subject to withholding, your final Q4 estimated tax payment is due.

January 31 – Deadline to Receive W-2s and 1099s

Schools and clients must send your wage and income statements by this date. Watch for:

- W-2s from your university
- 1099-NEC forms for speaking, camps, or side gigs
- 1099-Rs if you took any retirement withdrawals

FEBRUARY

Early February – Contract Renewal Review (Check Your Agreement)

Many coaching contracts require the institution to notify you by a specific date (often in February) of intent to renew, extend, or non-renew your deal.

Start Gathering Tax Documents

Begin organizing receipts, deductions, and retirement contributions for tax filing or your CPA.

MARCH

Mid-to-Late March – University Benefits Review Begins (Varies by School)

Start reviewing options for:

- Health insurance changes
- Dependent coverage
- Retirement contribution adjustments

March 15 – S-Corp and Partnership Tax Filing Deadline (if applicable)

If you've formed an LLC taxed as an S-Corp for camp income or side business, this is your tax return deadline unless you file for an extension.

APRIL

April 1 – Required Minimum Distributions Begin (if age 73+)

For coaches past retirement age with IRAs or 403(b)s, this is the deadline to take your first RMD.

April 15 – Federal Tax Filing Deadline

- Personal income tax return due
- First quarterly estimated tax payment due for current year
- Deadline to contribute to prior year's Roth IRA or Traditional IRA

April 15 – Deadline to File for an Extension (Form 4868)

If you need more time to file your return, request an automatic extension.

JUNE

June 15 – 2nd Quarterly Estimated Tax Payment Due

This applies if you're receiving 1099 income from camps, consulting, or training without tax withholding.

Mid-Year Review

Great time to:

- Review tax withholdings on your W-2
- Adjust your 403(b) or 457(b) contributions
- Evaluate summer camp income and set aside taxes

SEPTEMBER

September 15 – 3rd Quarterly Estimated Tax Payment Due

Also the deadline to file extended S-Corp or partnership returns if you filed an extension in March.

Start Contract and Compensation Review

Fall is often when departments start discussing contract extensions, renewals, or staff evaluations. Start gathering data on your performance, market value, and bonus eligibility.

OCTOBER

October 1–31 – Open Enrollment for University Benefits (Varies by School)

Enroll or make changes to health insurance, life insurance, FSA/HSA contributions, and dependent care plans.

October 15 – Deadline for Extended Individual Tax Returns

If you filed an extension back in April, your final return is due now.

NOVEMBER

Pre-Holiday Financial Planning Check-In

- Maximize remaining retirement contributions
- Finalize year-end charitable giving or business deductions
- Plan for final quarter estimated tax payments

DECEMBER

December 31 – End-of-Year Financial Deadlines

- Last day to contribute to 403(b) or 457(b) for the calendar year
- Take any required minimum distributions
- Complete charitable donations
- Use FSA funds before they expire
- Finalize any end-of-year bonuses or deferred compensation elections

BONUS TIPS:

- **Camp Income Planning:** If you run summer camps, track your income and expenses starting in **May or June**, and set aside 25–30% for taxes.
- **Contract Anniversary Date:** Know the exact date your contract was signed or takes effect. Renegotiation, evaluation, and benefits vesting often tie to this timeline.

Final Whistle:

You manage schedules and details for your team—do the same for your money. Put these dates on your calendar, set reminders, and work with a CPA or advisor to stay organized and ahead of the game. Because missed deadlines can cost you—and smart timing can *pay* you.

List of Questions to Ask During Contract Negotiations

Compensation & Salary Structure

- What is the base salary, and how frequently is it paid?
- Are there annual raises or cost-of-living adjustments built into the contract?
- What types of performance bonuses are available (e.g., postseason, academic success, conference titles)?
- Are signing bonuses, retention bonuses, or deferred compensation included?
- How and when are bonuses paid, and how are they taxed?

Contract Term and Renewal

- What is the official length of the contract?
- Are there automatic renewal clauses or performance-based extensions?
- What is the process and timeline for renegotiation or renewal?
- Is there language addressing mid-contract reviews or early extensions?
- What happens if no new agreement is signed when the current term ends?

Termination and Buyouts

- What are the terms if I am terminated without cause?
- How is "cause" defined in this agreement, and is the language clearly limited and specific?
- If terminated, is there a guaranteed buyout? How is it calculated?
- Does the contract contain an offset clause if I take another job?
- Are there protections in place to secure a portion of income or benefits after departure?

Benefits and Perks

- What health insurance plans are offered? Does coverage extend to my spouse and children?
- Is life insurance, long-term disability, or supplemental insurance included?
- What retirement plans are available (403(b), 457(b), pension)? Does the university contribute?
- Are there housing or vehicle allowances or stipends?
- Does the contract allow me to retain camp income or outside consulting revenue?

Professional and Personal Support

- Will the school pay for professional development, coaching clinics, or continuing education?
- Can I negotiate a financial planning stipend or access to a CPA or advisor?
- Are there relocation expenses covered for me and my family?
- Is spousal or family travel included for postseason or team events?
- Is there tuition assistance or access to university benefits for family members?

Other Contractual Considerations

- Can parts of the contract (e.g., bonuses or deferred pay) be structured to minimize tax burden?
- What liability protections or legal coverage is offered if I face job-related disputes?
- Can any part of the contract be tied to equity-building, like real estate or retirement investment vehicles?
- What are the expectations around social media, branding, or NIL-related activities?
- Will I receive an annual contract summary or breakdown for financial planning?

Final Tip: Never be afraid to ask questions during contract negotiations. The answers reveal not only the terms of your employment—but how much the institution truly values you, your time, and your long-term well-being. Get everything in writing, and when in doubt, have a trusted professional review the deal before you sign.

Glossary of Financial and Contract Terms

1. 403(b) Plan

A retirement savings plan available to employees of public schools and certain nonprofits. Similar to a 401(k), contributions are made pre-tax and grow tax-deferred.

2. 457(b) Plan

Another type of retirement plan for public sector employees. It allows for additional contributions and may offer more flexible withdrawal options.

3. Annuity

A financial product that provides a stream of income over time, often used for retirement planning.

4. Base Salary

The guaranteed annual salary outlined in a coaching contract, not including bonuses or incentives.

5. Bonus (Performance Bonus)

Extra compensation awarded for meeting specific goals such as winning seasons, academic benchmarks, or tournament success.

6. Buyout Clause

A provision in a contract that outlines the financial penalty or terms if a coach or employer ends the agreement early.

7. Cost-of-Living Adjustment (COLA)

An increase in salary designed to keep up with inflation.

8. Deferred Compensation

Earnings that are paid out at a later date, often used for tax planning or retention purposes.

9. Disability Insurance

Coverage that replaces a portion of income if you're unable to work due to illness or injury.

10. Emergency Fund

Savings set aside to cover unexpected expenses, usually 3–6 months of living costs.

11. Estate Planning

Preparing legal documents such as a will, trust, or power of attorney to manage your assets and wishes in the event of death or incapacitation.

12. Fringe Benefits

Non-cash compensation such as housing, vehicle stipends, health insurance, or tuition assistance.

13. Gross Pay

Total earnings before any deductions (taxes, insurance, retirement contributions).

14. Net Pay

The amount of money received after deductions—your "take-home" pay.

15. Offset Clause

A contract provision that reduces a buyout payout if the coach secures another job during the remaining contract period.

16. Pension

A fixed retirement income provided by some public institutions, often based on years of service and final salary.

17. Power of Attorney (POA)

A legal document allowing someone to make financial or medical decisions on your behalf.

18. Rollover (Retirement Account)

Moving funds from one retirement account to another (e.g., from a 403(b) at your old school to an IRA) without triggering taxes or penalties.

19. Signing Bonus

A one-time payment received upon signing a new contract or extension.

20. Termination Clause

Section of a contract outlining conditions under which either party can end the agreement, with or without cause.

21. Vesting

The process of earning full ownership of employer contributions to a retirement plan over time.

22. Will

A legal document that specifies how your assets should be distributed after death.

23. LLC (Limited Liability Company)

A business structure that separates personal and business assets, often used by coaches for camps, consulting, or other side income.

24. Sole Proprietor

A simple business structure where the coach is personally responsible for all income and liabilities. Common for those earning side income from camps or clinics.

25. Tax-Deferred

Income or investments where taxes are postponed until withdrawal (e.g., in a 403(b) or traditional IRA).

26. Roth IRA

A retirement account funded with after-tax dollars. Withdrawals in retirement are tax-free if certain conditions are met.

27. Morality Clause (Conduct Clause)

A contract term that allows for termination if the coach engages in behavior deemed damaging to the institution's reputation.

28. Retention Bonus

A financial incentive paid for completing a certain term of a contract or staying with a program through specific milestones.

29. Consulting Income

Earnings from professional advising or speaking engagements outside of your primary employer. Often paid as 1099 income.

30. Umbrella Insurance

Extra liability insurance that provides coverage beyond the limits of homeowners, auto, or other policies. Helpful for protecting assets as income grows.

Retirement Plan Consolidation Checklist

For College Coaches Navigating Multiple Jobs, Plans, and Providers

Over a career that may span five or more schools, you could accumulate several 403(b), 457(b), pension, or IRA accounts. Consolidating your retirement accounts can simplify management, reduce fees, and ensure you have a clear view of your financial future.

Use this checklist to guide the consolidation process:

1. Identify All Existing Retirement Accounts

- ❑ Gather a list of every school or employer where you had a retirement plan
- ❑ Locate old 403(b), 457(b), 401(k), or pension plan statements
- ❑ Check for traditional IRAs or Roth IRAs opened during transitions
- ❑ Contact HR departments of previous employers for plan access or details

2. Log In and Review Each Account

- ❑ Confirm the current account balance and investment allocations
- ❑ Note the type of account (403(b), 457(b), IRA, pension, etc.)
- ❑ Review fees, performance, and available investment options
- ❑ Check beneficiary designations and update as needed

3. Evaluate Which Accounts Should Be Consolidated

- ❑ Determine which accounts can legally be merged (e.g., 403(b) → IRA)
- ❑ Decide if it makes sense to consolidate into your current employer's plan or into a personal IRA
- ❑ Evaluate tax implications of any rollover
- ❑ Consider future flexibility, investment choices, and advisor access

4. Choose the Right Rollover Destination

- ❑ Traditional IRA (flexible, often lower fees, broader investment options)
- ❑ Roth IRA (after-tax rollover option; may trigger taxes)
- ❑ Your current school's 403(b) or 457(b) plan (may allow roll-ins)
- ❑ Employer-sponsored pension—check if it can be rolled or should be left untouched

5. Request a Direct Rollover

- ❑ Contact the old plan provider and request a **direct rollover** (not a distribution)
- ❑ Complete necessary paperwork for both the old and new plan providers
- ❑ Have the check made payable to the **new provider** (not to you personally)
- ❑ Confirm receipt of funds in the new account

6. Reinvest and Rebalance

- ❑ Choose your new investment options
- ❑ Align with your current risk tolerance, age, and retirement timeline
- ❑ Set automatic contributions (if applicable)
- ❑ Rebalance at least annually

7. Keep Records and Stay Organized

- ❑ Retain copies of all rollover confirmations
- ❑ Save the most recent statement from the closed account for future reference
- ❑ Note the date and amount of each rollover for tax reporting purposes
- ❑ Create a digital or physical retirement folder

8. Work with a Professional

- ❑ Consult a financial advisor or CPA to:
- Avoid rollover mistakes and penalties
- Minimize fees and taxes
- Maximize retirement income planning
- Strategically withdraw or convert funds in the future

Bonus Tip: Set a Recurring Review

- ❑ Revisit your retirement accounts once a year
- ❑ Check beneficiaries after major life changes
- ❑ Adjust your savings rate as your income grows

Consolidating your retirement plans isn't just about simplification—it's about **control**, **clarity**, and **confidence** in your long-term financial game plan.

Sample Coaching Contract Breakdown

Understanding the Structure and Language Behind the Offer

Below is a sample structure of a head coaching contract at a mid-sized university. While actual terms vary widely by level and institution, this example helps illustrate what you might expect—and what to look out for.

1. Position and Term

Language:

Coach is hired as Head Coach of Men's Basketball at Midstate University for a term of 3 years, beginning July 1, 2025 and ending June 30, 2028.

Explanation:

Defines the role and how long the contract is valid. Also sets the employment start and end dates.

2. Base Salary

Language:

Coach shall receive a base salary of $175,000 per year, payable in bi-weekly installments in accordance with university payroll.

Explanation:

This is your guaranteed pay. It's what you'll get regardless of wins/losses or bonuses. Paid on a regular schedule like other university staff.

3. Incentives and Bonuses

Language:

Coach may receive additional compensation as follows:

- $10,000 for a conference championship
- $5,000 for an NCAA Tournament appearance
- $2,000 for a team GPA above 3.0
- $5,000 for completing the full term of contract (retention bonus)

Explanation:

Outlines performance-based and loyalty incentives. Important to ask whether these are automatic, how they're taxed, and when they're paid.

4. Benefits

Language:

Coach shall be entitled to university benefits, including health insurance, dental and vision plans, participation in the 403(b) retirement plan, life and disability insurance, and tuition assistance for dependents.

Explanation:

Defines the coach's eligibility for benefits available to university employees. These can represent significant value beyond the base salary.

5. Additional Perks

Language:

Coach will receive a university-leased vehicle, a $1,000 monthly housing stipend, and five complimentary season tickets for each home game.

Explanation:

Perks vary but can include housing, vehicles, travel, gear, or family benefits. These may be taxable, so check with a CPA.

6. Camp Income

Language:

Coach may operate summer camps using university facilities. Coach will retain 90% of net camp income and must file an annual camp financial report.

Explanation:

Some contracts allow coaches to profit from running camps—others may split or restrict it. Understand who owns the revenue and what facilities cost.

7. Termination Clause

Language:

The University may terminate Coach without cause and must pay 75% of the remaining base salary at time of termination. If terminated for cause (including conduct violations or NCAA infractions), no payout shall be made.

Explanation:

Details what happens if the university ends the contract. "Without cause" means you're still owed money. "With cause" means you lose it. Understand how "cause" is defined.

8. Coach-Initiated Buyout

Language:

If Coach terminates the contract before the expiration date, Coach shall pay the University $25,000 in liquidated damages.

Explanation:

This is your buyout—what you owe the school if you leave early. Some are flat-rate, others are prorated or negotiable.

9. Conduct and Morality Clause

Language:

Coach agrees to maintain standards of conduct consistent with University policies and public expectations. Any behavior deemed damaging to the institution's reputation may result in termination for cause.

Explanation:

These clauses are common and often vague. It's critical to understand what "conduct unbecoming" includes—and if you can be terminated for off-field behavior or social media activity.

10. Renewal and Extension Language

Language:

This agreement may be renewed by mutual consent prior to the end of the term. Coach will be notified by February 1, 2028, regarding the University's intent to renew.

Explanation:

Sets the timeline for contract renewal discussions. Ask for clear dates to protect yourself from being left in limbo at the end of a term.

11. Outside Income and Appearances

Language:

Coach may accept speaking engagements, consulting work, and media appearances with prior written approval. All outside income must be disclosed annually.

Explanation:

Schools often want transparency if you're earning money beyond your base pay. Clarify what's allowed and what needs approval.

12. Governing Law

Language:

This agreement shall be governed by the laws of the State of [State Name].

Explanation:

Determines what legal system will oversee the contract in case of a dispute. Usually tied to the university's state.

Final Tip:

Always review your contract with a sports attorney or experienced financial advisor. Contracts are more than just salary—they impact your stability, freedom, and long-term security.

Let me know if you'd like this formatted as a visual sample page, worksheet, or added to an appendix with commentary for further reading.

Questions to ask professionals

10 Questions to Ask a Financial Advisor

1. Are you a fiduciary 100% of the time?
2. How are you compensated—fee-only, commission-based, or a combination?
3. What certifications do you hold (e.g., CFP, CFA, ChFC)?
4. Do you have experience working with clients in athletics or entertainment?
5. How will you help me plan for taxes, retirement, and investing?
6. What's your investment philosophy?
7. Can you help me with budgeting, insurance, and estate planning?
8. How often will we meet, and how do you communicate?
9. What happens if I decide to end the relationship—are there any penalties?
10. Can I see a sample financial plan you've created (with personal info removed)?

10 Questions to Ask a CPA (Certified Public Accountant)

1. Do you work with clients who earn variable or self-employment income like coaching bonuses or consulting fees?
2. How do you stay current with tax laws, especially around NIL, 1099 income, and business deductions?
3. Can you help with quarterly estimated tax payments?
4. Do you offer tax planning, or just tax preparation?

5. What's your process for reviewing deductions and maximizing legal write-offs?
6. How will you help me if I'm audited?
7. Do you file in multiple states? (Important for coaches who move often)
8. What tax software or platform do you use, and can I access copies easily?
9. Can you coordinate with my financial advisor or legal team?
10. What do you charge, and is that an annual fee or hourly rate?

10 Questions to Ask When Hiring an Agent

1. What is your experience representing coaches (or athletes) in contract negotiations?
2. How do you charge for your services—flat fee, retainer, percentage?
3. Will you negotiate only my base salary, or also perks like housing, buyouts, and bonuses?
4. Do you have relationships with athletic directors or university administrators?
5. What is your communication style, and how often will we talk?
6. Will you review and advise on endorsement, consulting, or media deals?
7. Do you have any conflicts of interest (e.g., representing multiple coaches at the same school)?
8. Can I talk to some of your current or former clients?
9. What's your philosophy when it comes to negotiating contracts—aggressive, relational, or balanced?
10. Will you work with my attorney or financial advisor as part of my overall team?

10 Questions to Ask When Hiring a Business Manager

1. What types of clients do you typically work with (athletes, entertainers, business owners)?
2. How do you get paid—monthly retainer, percentage of income, or project-based fees?
3. What services do you offer—bookkeeping, bill pay, financial reports, budgeting?
4. How do you handle cash flow for clients with inconsistent income?
5. Can you track and categorize all sources of income (NIL, camps, speaking, side businesses)?
6. Will you help with business formation, taxes, and expense tracking for my LLC or side hustle?
7. Do you work with my CPA and financial advisor to keep everyone aligned?
8. What financial reports do I receive, and how often?
9. How do you ensure my data and information is secure?
10. Can you provide references or case studies of clients similar to me?

Financial Literacy Questions for Student-Athletes:

These questions can help foster valuable conversations with student-athletes and open the door to providing them with the financial education they need to navigate the complexities of NIL and their personal finances.

1. **Do you currently have a budget or track your spending in any way? If not, would you be open to learning how to do this?**
2. **Have you ever heard of NIL (Name, Image, and Likeness) and how it can affect your income as a student-athlete?**
3. **What are some ways you think you could use your personal brand to make money as a student-athlete?**
4. **Do you understand how taxes work when you start earning money through NIL?**
5. **What are the biggest financial challenges you're facing right now as a student-athlete?**
6. **Have you considered opening a savings account or investing your earnings?**
7. **What financial goals do you have for the next 1-3 years?**
8. **Do you have any student loans or credit card debt? How are you managing them?**
9. **Have you talked to anyone about how NIL earnings could impact your eligibility for scholarships or financial aid?**
10. **Are you familiar with the concept of compound interest and how it can help your money grow over time?**

11. **Have you set up any long-term savings plans, like for retirement or future investments?**
12. **What are some examples of financial mistakes you've made or seen other athletes make?**
13. **Do you know the difference between gross income and net income, and how taxes affect the amount you take home?**
14. **Are you aware of how to protect your income, such as using insurance or setting up a business entity for your NIL deals?**
15. **What would you do if you received a large lump sum of money from an NIL deal?**
16. **Do you understand the importance of credit scores and how they can impact your financial decisions in the future?**
17. **Do you have a financial advisor or anyone guiding you on your financial decisions?**
18. **Are you familiar with the various types of insurance that could protect you (health, disability, life insurance) while you're a student-athlete?**
19. **How do you plan on using any money you make through NIL deals—are you saving, investing, or spending it?**
20. **Have you had any conversations with your parents or guardians about financial planning or NIL earnings?**
21. **What financial habits do you think are essential for long-term success as an athlete, even after your playing career is over?**
22. **Are you aware of the potential risks of signing contracts or agreements with brands for NIL deals?**
23. **Have you considered using any financial apps or tools to help you manage your money better?**
24. **What is your plan for managing NIL income if you move to a new state or country to play?**
25. **If you had to manage all of your NIL earnings by yourself, what do you think would be the most challenging part of doing so?**

Made in the USA
Monee, IL
04 November 2026

67387588R00157